# Cry *from the* Mountains

# Cry *from the* Mountains

*To Eric & Sherry Allen*
*Thank you for your service*

*Keith Decker*

Keith Decker
with
Joyce Sweeney Martin

*John 12:32*

authorHOUSE®

*AuthorHouse™*
*1663 Liberty Drive*
*Bloomington, IN 47403*
*www.authorhouse.com*
*Phone: 1 (800) 839-8640*

*Published by AuthorHouse 05/12/2015*

*ISBN: 978-1-5049-1159-7 (sc)*
*ISBN: 978-1-5049-1160-3 (e)*

*Print information available on the last page.*

*KJV*
*Scripture quotations marked KJV are from the Holy Bible, King James Version
(Authorized Version). First published in 1611. Quoted from the KJV Classic
Reference Bible, Copyright © 1983 by The <u>Zondervan</u> Corporation.*

*NIV*
*Scripture portions marked NIV are from the Holy Bible, New International Version.*

# Contents

# Foreword

Keith and I had been out visiting people who have been helped through Cedaridge Ministries when we stopped at a fast-food restaurant in Williamsburg, Kentucky, for a bite to eat. While we were eating, a middle-aged man and woman came by our table to say hello to Keith. After Keith introduced the couple to me, the man immediately began talking about how Keith had influenced his life.

It seems that when Keith was a young man, he had begun a church-sponsored softball team for boys in a rural community near Williamsburg, and this man had been one of the boys on that team. The man simply couldn't say enough good things about what Keith had done. He said Keith not only had given those boys something to do that summer, but he also had shown them that with hard work and a sense of purpose, they could be successful no matter what their circumstances were. He said that summer those young lads learned to work as a team and were successful beyond their wildest dreams – the team finished second in their league.

The man went on to say that he and his wife had become successful business people and that their company, which is based in Williamsburg, has expanded to serve clients in more than forty states. He credited Keith's interest in him as a teenager for giving him the confidence to build the business. He went on to name at least seven other men who had been on that softball team who, like him, now have flourishing careers. Then he and his wife told Keith they wanted to help Cedaridge Ministries in any way they can.

As I reflected on the hours I'd spent with Keith that day, I was reminded that almost every time I've been with Keith over the sixteen years I've known him, I've met people whose lives he has touched. And I gave thanks to the Lord that Keith has always tackled the immediate need and then left the long-term results in the hands of the Lord – even when the need was to start a softball team.

Meeting needs. Touching lives in the name of Jesus. Giving God all the glory. That is Keith Decker.

Larry Martin
Minister
Louisville, Kentucky
May 2015

# Preface

For twenty-three years, my wife Joyce and I have ministered to impoverished people in the Appalachian Mountains of Eastern Kentucky through Cedaridge Ministries located in Williamsburg, Kentucky. And for most of those years, Cedaridge has flown under the radar. We've tried to be faithful in meeting needs but haven't spent much time telling the story of what the Lord has been doing. That changed, however, in February 2012 when the Lord told me that all the things that had happened in the previous twenty years of Cedaridge's history were only a taste of what He was going to do in the future. Among other things, He told me He would make known to His people the vision Cedaridge has had from the beginning and would show them what He has done, is doing, and will do in the future through the ministry.

I also believe the Lord wants my own growing-up experiences to be told at this time. If you are facing seemingly impossible life circumstances and need a word of hope, this book is for you. I am living proof you have a chance for a meaningful life no matter what. There are people who care, and if you will trust and search for the Lord He will help you get connected to them. You can be the one in your family who can change the direction for generations to come – and you can do that only through knowing and living for the Lord. Granted, it won't be a simple process because He will change you from the inside, but that change will lay the foundation for every decision you will make from that time forward. As long as you give the Lord something to work with, He will make you into someone of whom you will be proud.

As for the book title *Cry from the Mountains*, in my senior year of high school many years ago the Lord gave me the title and planted the dream for a book in my heart. Looking back, I can see clearly why He wanted that title. As you read the book, I believe you will see why, too.

In His timing, the Lord put writer Joyce Sweeney Martin in my path in 2014. Over the next months, she worked tirelessly to put words to the thoughts of my heart and to write the story of how God has directed my life and how He has worked through Cedaridge. Thank you, Joyce

Thank you to every volunteer who has worked with my wife, Joyce, and me at Cedaridge over the years; I wish I could name each of you. Thank you to everyone who gave permission for their stories to be told. (I take responsibility for any omissions or mistakes.) Thank you to every person who has done so much to help me over my almost sixty years of life.

Keith Decker
Williamsburg, Kentucky
May 2015

# One

One cold, snowy Kentucky morning in early December 1972, I woke up at about six o'clock, expecting the day to be just like every other day in the Decker household. By the time nightfall came, however, my life had irrevocably changed.

Late that afternoon my oldest brother, William, told me he and I were going to ride over to see one of our mother's sisters. When he dropped me off at the end of the lane leading to her house, I fully expected him to pick me up later that day. He didn't.

Looking back, being dropped off at my aunt's house brought everything to a head. Over the previous years, I'd had to spend many nights with friends in order to stay in school. When I was in the seventh and eighth grades, I'd often stayed with other people, including my basketball coach, after late school activities because my house was too far from school for me to walk home after nightfall. And when I'd started high school in 1971, I'd had no permanent place to live and had just gone from friend to friend while trying to stay in school, which was located twenty miles from my home. Thankfully, through the years people who knew my home situation had looked after me. They had known there were lots of distractions to keep me from doing well in school and they had wanted to help, although I'm not sure I realized that at the time.

Somewhere along the way I'd begun to want a different lifestyle than that of my family. As I saw how my friends lived, I wanted a life resembling theirs. My friends' families also sensed I wanted something more. In fact, just a week before that fateful December day, two neighbors had told me that if I ever expected to amount to anything then I needed to get away from my family. I remember thinking I wasn't sure I had the courage to make such a drastic break.

Being left at my aunt's house forced the break. Looking back, I know it was the first in a series of God-orchestrated events that forever changed the course of my life.

I FULLY EXPECTED William to come back for me. Each day for a week, I watched for him to return. When he failed to show up, I finally set out walking home to try to find out what was going on.

Snow still covered the ground, and the air was bitterly cold as I walked… and walked…and walked up the holler/hollow. When I got to our house, my family – including William – was gone!

I crawled in a window, looked around, and immediately realized that no one had been in the house for several days. Even though our furniture was still in place, there was no fire in the heating stove and the ashes were cold; plus, there was no evidence any food had been prepared for days. It seemed everybody had just picked up and left. What to do? My few clothes were still there, so I stuffed a pair of pants and a shirt into a brown paper bag, and I left, too.

By that time dusk was settling in and the temperature had dropped even more. Where had my family gone? What was I going to do?

All I knew to do was to set out walking once again. As I thought about my situation, I asked myself, *"What if I fell into a black hole tonight?"*

And then I answered my own question: *"Nobody would even miss me."*

To be clear, my mother and stepfather didn't throw me out, but they did leave me behind. In our Kentucky Appalachian culture in the 1970s, it wasn't unusual for a family to pick up and do its own thing, leaving sons or daughters behind. In fact, often when a child turned sixteen he or she was expected to move out of the family home, which was made even easier by the fact that by Kentucky law a student could drop out of school at age sixteen. I was already seventeen.

Of course, the day my family picked up and moved from that rental house that had been our home for about a year, they knew I wasn't at home and they knew I wouldn't know where they'd gone. They did abandon me.

Two years later I learned why they'd moved away so quickly and left me behind. By December 1972, Mom, her husband (Steve Love), one of my brothers and his wife, and I had been the only people living at home.

All my other siblings and step-siblings had married and moved on. One brother and his family had moved to North Carolina, so my family had suddenly decided to join them there. Actually, moving seemed to be in our DNA as for most years of the previous decade we'd moved several times. Never, however, had we moved out of state. (I'd attended three elementary schools in eight years, moving back and forth between them several times depending on where we were living. In spite of everything, I made the all-tournament basketball team at Oak Grove Elementary.)

THAT WASN'T THE first time I'd been left by my family: My father had given me away when I was just six months old. This is how the story was told to me as I was growing up:

While I'd been a healthy baby at birth, by my sixth month I'd developed pneumonia and was severely malnourished. With six other children to see to and with my mom sick at the time, my dad felt he couldn't care for me and decided to give me away to someone who could.

Again, the reader must remember that in the 1950s in Appalachia, giving a child away wasn't uncommon. Like my family, many families had more children than they could see to and often would ask someone in the community to take one or more children. My dad knew that – and he also knew the custom called for a parent to go to the local country store and plead his or her case. So that is exactly what he did.

That December day, as usual several people were gathered around the old coal-burning stove when Dad joined them. He told the group that his wife was sick and in the hospital, that he had seven children, that he was having trouble feeding all of them, and that he needed help with the youngest, a six-month-old son named Keith.

"Will anyone take Keith?" my dad asked.

That morning, a nurse named Gladys Mullis had come to the store. Immediately she said, "Yes, I'll take Keith." Later that day when she came to our house to pick me up, Gladys quickly saw how sick I was, so she bundled me up and took me straight to a doctor. I was told that when Ole Doctor Keith Smith – as he was called – examined me, he told Gladys, "This baby's too sick; he won't live." Remember, this was 1955 and medical treatment was limited.

Defying the doctor's advice, Gladys responded, "I don't care what I have to do, I'll not lose this baby."

Gladys, her husband, and their two teenage daughters took me in for about six months. They even wanted to adopt me, but by that time Mom was healthier. Plus, when she'd found out Dad had given me away she'd been furious and wanted me back. The day Mom came to get me, Gladys' daughters hid me; they didn't want to give me back, but, of course, they did.

Looking back, I harbor no ill will toward my dad. I know he had no choice. Dad could have let me die; instead, he wanted to at least give me a chance. Looking back, I know God was stepping in to save me – as He would continue to do so many times over the next years. I also know God was watching over me when a nurse named Gladys said "Yes" that day.

And I harbor no ill will toward my family for leaving me behind when I was seventeen. They knew I'd already started living by different values than theirs. Church, school, and high ethical and moral standards had become important to me. For example, each Sunday morning I would get up early, put on my not-so-nice clothes, and walk to church while they stayed in bed. From the time I first began attending Baptist churches, I loved everything about church and wanted to attend every time the doors were open. Additionally, while all my siblings, step siblings, and half siblings had dropped out of school by age sixteen, I was trying hard to stay in school. I already wanted a better life.

WHILE MOM DID her best to raise us right, it's an understatement to say that our family life was less than ideal. Mom (nee, Hettie Mable "Hettie" Walters) and her first husband, James Gilbert Hensley, had six children; Hensley, however, had been married twice before he married Mom and had thirty children by his first two wives. After Hensley died, Mom married John "Jack" William Decker; I was the seventh of their eight children. After she and my dad divorced, Mom married Steve Love, who already had fifteen children. Mom and Mr. Love had no children. The best I can count, I am one of fifty-nine full, half, and step brothers and sisters.

At one time, fourteen of my family members lived in a four-room, 15' x 20' house, which was located on Hensley's seventy-five acre farm up a holler six miles from a gravel road and just above the Grove community in Whitley County, Kentucky. The farm had become Mom's upon Hensley's death, which created enormous friction between their children and Hensley's other children. It was the house where I lived from the time of my birth until I was about eight years old, I think.

Of all Mom's fourteen children, I was the only one born in a hospital, which wouldn't have happened without the sacrifice made by my eldest half-brother, John Henry "Johnny" Hensley. At age seventeen, he intentionally had moved to Idaho to work on a farm in order to send money back home so Mom could give birth to me in Corbin Hospital in Corbin, Kentucky. Years later, family members told me Johnny had seen how much Mom had struggled over the years, and he wanted her safely to give birth in a hospital. They told me because work opportunities were few and far between in our area, Johnny knew he needed to move away to make money. Plus, because Johnny was Mormon, he chose to move to Idaho with its large Mormon population. Sadly, three months before I was born, he died of leukemia at age eighteen. Mom flew to Idaho for the funeral. When she returned home, she continued working in the fields in order to provide for her family, as she had always done. In fact, the day before I was born, she worked all day. That night, she went to the hospital. I was born the next morning at 5 a.m. It was Sunday, July 31, 1955. She named me Keith Edward Decker.

Throughout my growing-up years our family was poor by anybody's standards. At one of the places where we lived Mom cooked our meager meals in the fireplace that also served as our only heat source. (To be honest, often in elementary school the only food I had to eat for an evening meal was ketchup that I saved from free school lunches.) All through the years, she did our laundry – or "washin'" as we called it – on a washboard in water we carried from a spring. Our clothes were hand-me-downs. And of course, there was never any indoor plumbing, just an outhouse outback. All in all, it was a hardscrabble life.

When I was six years old, Mom and Dad separated. Their five oldest children – two girls and three boys – went to live with Dad, and the three youngest, who were boys (including me), stayed with Mom. They divorced when I was twelve. For the next ten years, I saw Dad about once a month. I remember spending one summer with him when he was living with my brother David. By then he had grown old and feeble and I helped take care of him. You see, he was fifty years old and Mom was twenty-seven when they married. He died in 1971 when I was sixteen. For a long time after Dad's death, I found it hard to sleep at night. I even kept his obituary from the local newspaper. Finally, I burned the clippings in the fireplace, hoping to find some peace. Only after I got saved did I begin to realize what I was looking for was the peace only God can give.

As for her religious faith, Mom had become a Mormon when she married Mr. Hensley and continued in the Mormon faith after she married my dad. I don't think she was a serious Mormon. Instead, I think she took things at face value and didn't delve into the deeper tenets of Mormonism. Hers was a simple, personal faith. Because Mormonism preached strong moral and ethical values, it was okay with her. Elders of our Mormon church often came to our home to teach. What I remember most is their clear teachings about right and wrong. To this day, I appreciate the moral foundation they laid out for me. (I also remember that the best meals we had in our house were served when the Mormon elders came to visit.)

Some of my favorite memories of Mom involve thunderstorms. As the thunder rolled, Mom would sit in her rocking chair, gather my two brothers and me around her, and sing about how God talks in the thunder. The way she sang and talked about God was so precious. He was very real to her.

NOW IT WAS DECEMBER 1972, seventeen years into my life. I was homeless, cold, hungry, and seemingly hopeless. As I walked and thought about how no one would miss me if I just disappeared, something miraculous happened. Very clearly I felt something slap me on the chest and say, *"Quit thinking that way."* In later years, I would know that "something" was Someone – God. That night, I had a "me-and-the-Lord experience" – one of many I've had through the years since. That night, the Lord placed a ray of hope for the future in me. Even though I didn't know it at the time, He heard my cry from the mountains.

That snowy, cold December night as I continued to walk and think about my predicament, I suddenly remembered how an elderly couple who lived up the road from my family's house had always told me that if I needed a place to sleep I could come to their house. I made my way there only to see that the house lights were off. I knew that meant the couple had already gone to bed. I didn't want to wake them. What was I going to do?

Then I remembered that my Sunday School teacher at Greenland Baptist Church, Mrs. Eula Sears, lived across the road. I decided to ask her for help. I'd never felt bad about asking help from anybody who said they loved the Lord – and I knew she did. I believed if Jesus said it in the

Bible and if a person loves the Lord, then he or she will do what Jesus said. I knew Jesus had said His followers should take in the stranger and give food to the hungry; therefore, I had no fear in asking Mrs. Sears for help.

Because of how I understood Scripture, I wasn't surprised when I asked Mrs. Sears if she would care if I came in to warm my hands and she immediately invited me in. I went in – and then I looked down at myself and saw how dirty I was. I looked at Mrs. Sears' clean living room with its nice furniture and I just couldn't bring my dirty self to sit down. (Before I'd walked home, I'd helped my cousin strip a car; I was covered in dirt and grease.) So I asked her if I could wash my hands. She replied with something that did amaze me. I remember her exact words: "Keith," she said, "I've been trying to figure out a way to ask you to take a bath without hurting your feelings." She told me she would be happy to wash my clothes while I took a bath. It was a deal.

Man, that bath water was the hottest water! It felt so good. I looked like a red lobster as I came out of that water – not that I knew what a lobster was back then. And I had clean clothes to boot. Now I could be comfortable sitting in one of her chairs!

After my bath, Mrs. Sears fixed me a meal. After I ate, I was so tired that I fell asleep in that chair. When her husband came home, I woke up. Then they asked me to stay the night.

The lessons of that one night have stayed with me until this day. That night, I experienced the meaning of Jesus' admonition first-hand. Jesus' words came alive for me. Because of what I experienced, I would never forget what it's like to be homeless, hungry, and seemingly hopeless. I would never forget what it's like to have a believer in Jesus take a person in and by that simple act give them hope. Because of that night, the Lord placed in me a life-long commitment to follow His command given in Matthew 25:35-36 to feed the hungry, clothe the naked, visit the prisoner, and most importantly of all, to bring people to faith in Jesus as Savior and Lord.

The next day I was back on the streets, so to speak; actually, I was back on the gravel country roads of Whitley County. It was Wednesday, so that night I went to the weekly prayer meeting at Greenland church. When the pastor asked for personal testimonies at the end of the service, I told the congregation I had no place to live and asked if anybody had a place where I could stay. They were all good people, but as they left after the service one by one they just said, "I'll pray for you." As the number of people dwindled, I began to wonder if anyone would take me in. Finally, the poorest family in the church said I could stay with them. That night I went home with the Chambers family and stayed for three days, during which time another big snow fell and blocked all the roads.

I remember thinking that if I didn't have some stability in my life by Christmas break, there was a good chance I wouldn't finish school, and I would be devastated. As I've reflected on that time in my life and as I've faced other obstacles over the years, I've come to understand that God never lets His child get to the point of total devastation. I've learned by experience that when you are in a deep valley of despair and sense there's a deeper valley ahead you're trying to stay out of, God will never let you get to that second valley if you will trust Him. Instead, He will provide a way out. When you've done everything you can, God will show you the next valley to let you know that the current valley may seem hard, but it's nothing compared to the one that could be ahead. He wants you to focus on where you are at the moment, not on what might lie ahead.

That December my valley was to stand in front of the church members that Wednesday night, make my plight known, and then go home with any family who offered me a place to stay. That night, the deeper valley looming large in front of me – homelessness, dropping out of school, and everything I could have faced because of that – just disappeared.

For the first time in my life, I realized that many people were aware of my desperate situation and were willing to help me. That night, the Lord began to open doors both in my understanding of myself and in providing people who would help. Looking back, Mrs. Sears welcoming me in began my turn to a better life. Then the Chambers family from Greenland church who took me in added another solid piece. Over the next two and a half years, each person and each family who helped me added to my resolve to find a better life.

Like so many of the paths the Lord would make over the years, the next unfolded unexpectedly. When the roads finally cleared after the big snowstorm, the pastor and wife of Greenland Church came to visit me and to ask me to live with them. To tell the truth, I wasn't surprised by their offer because I knew Norman and Carol Alderman were God's people – and I believed that God's people always take care of those in need. Funny thing, however, I don't think I'd ever thought of myself as being in need. In spite of what I'd seen in other families, a huge part of me had just assumed that the way I lived was normal. Still, you really can't know what you don't have until you experience what others do have. During my time with the Aldermans, I experienced much of what I didn't have, which increased my appetite for a better life than the one I'd known.

INDEED, THE LORD continued to instill hope for my future during the five months I stayed with the Aldermans. They helped me figure out many things, including school. I was now in the second semester of my sophomore year at Whitley County High School in Williamsburg, but things weren't looking so good. The previous semester I'd missed twenty-four days and had racked up D's and F's on my report card. Because I'd turned sixteen a year and a half before, I knew that legally I could drop out. I didn't want to, but I had seriously considered it. Living with the Aldermans began to change all that.

At the Aldermans, for the first time I had help with school. They got me up early each day; they made sure I did my homework; and they made sure I attended school. In fact, during the semester I lived with them, I missed only four days and that was because I was sick. And I began making A's and B's.

Now at school, instead of my teachers saying they would give me a problem to do if I was in school, they began to see that whatever they offered me, I gladly took and ran with it. I'd never known they saw potential in me, but now I knew they did. How life can change when somebody encourages you! You don't need anyone to do the work for you; you just need someone to be an encourager. Those teachers saw something in me, and they began to jump in and help me. Soon I learned they even had begun to meet to talk about ways to help me. In fact, the same teachers who'd been ready to give up on me were now first in line to help – and they weren't even telling anyone about what they were doing; they just did it. I think they realized my situation hadn't been of my own doing; they realized I really wanted to do better but didn't know how.

That semester, the Lord used my teachers to show me how to make a better life, and I made a vow to do everything I could to "take the doors off the school" and take advantage of every opportunity that came my way. Looking back, in my mind it's a bit like Abraham when he separated from Lot in the story in Genesis 13. As soon as I separated from my past life, my life completely changed. The things I wanted to do no longer seemed difficult because so many people were available to help.

At the Aldermans, I also experienced a different home life than the one I'd known before. At home, Mom had talked a lot about God and had done her best, but at the Aldermans I got to be around people who followed Him in their daily lives. They were busy twenty-somethings. Carol was teaching in the preschool Head Start program, and Norm was working on his master's degree at nearby Union College and pastoring the church, but the foundation of their lives was God. Every day I saw them read the Bible and I listened to them talk about God. I watched them live out their faith. Until then, I'd seen the Christian life as an outsider looking in; now I was on the inside.

For the first time I also experienced what a loving church is like when the Aldermans got the congregation involved in caring for my physical and spiritual needs. To a young lad, it seemed as if all hundred or so members of Greenland church wanted to do something for me. For the first time I got to see church up close, and it began to grab hold of me. I eagerly embraced it all. I began reading my Bible more and became active in the church. I sang in my first duet and even was named volunteer youth leader at the church.

I was eager to do anything asked of me in the church, which led to at least one hilarious moment. One summer day during Vacation Bible School, Norman asked me to go get a woman and bring her to the church. I immediately took out walking. When I got to the woman's house, she came to the door, gathered up her purse, and then asked, "Where's the car?" Well, there was no car. So I – a seventeen-year-old boy – and she – an eighty-plus-year-old woman – started walking down U.S. 25 to the church. When Norman and the other people saw us coming, they burst out laughing. Of course, Norm asked, "Why didn't you take the car?" I replied, "You didn't say, 'Take the car.' You just said, 'Go get her.'"

DURING THE TIME I lived with the Aldermans, I began to think and talk seriously about what I wanted to do with my life. Even though I'd been baptized at age eight in the Mormon church in Corbin, I hadn't got saved until I was sixteen years old and in the eighth grade. At the time, I'd stayed off and on a few nights at a time with Geneva and Clayton Walters who recently had got saved at Cedar Gap Baptist Church in Buttermilk Hollow outside Corbin. To be honest, until that time I'd only gone to non-Mormon churches a couple of times, and I hadn't been favorably impressed. In fact, I'd even made fun of the emotional preachers I'd heard there.

Then the Walters invited me to Cedar Gap, and that church seemed different. Instead of an emotional sermon, I heard the word of salvation, the word that Jesus died for me.

When the invitation to accept salvation was given at the end of that Sunday morning worship service, I put out a fleece – even though I didn't know the term at the time. I bowed my head and asked God, *"If it's You, Lord, Who is speaking to me, let somebody come from the front of the sanctuary to me in my pew."*

When I looked up, I saw a man staring at me. Then he started moving from the front to the center of the aisle, never taking his eyes off me. I immediately got out of my pew, walked to the front and knelt at the altar and prayed, *"Lord, forgive me of my sins. Come into my life and save me."*

At that moment, it was like a hot poker was placed on my heart. Then I felt weak. For the first time as a young man, I cried. I felt free. A burden had been lifted from me. If someone had asked me what it all meant, I couldn't have explained, but I knew the experience was real. Later, I came to know the Spirit of the Lord had been working in me.

The preacher, Richard McKiddy, asked me if I wanted to be baptized that afternoon but I immediately said, "No." I was scared to death of what my mother would say. At lunch with the Walters, however, things changed. The Lord reminded me of an old country song about "walking that lonesome valley by yourself." I knew that I had to be baptized that day, no matter what anyone said. I heard the Lord say, *"This being baptized is something I want you to do, and you have to decide to do it or not without asking anyone else if it is okay."* Then and there I knew the Lord wanted me to be baptized – and only I could make that decision. I couldn't put it off on anyone else or ask if everybody was happy about it. It was enough that the Lord wanted me to be baptized.

And so that Sunday afternoon as Brother McKiddy was baptizing several other people in a local pond, I asked if I, too, could be baptized. As was the custom, McKiddy asked the church members who had come to the baptismal service to vote on the matter. Every hand went up. At that moment, I felt something I'd never felt before. Before then, most of what I'd ever heard said about me was "dirty boy" and "don't have anything to do with him" and other such things. Now, I was no longer an outcast; now I knew I belonged.

11

From that time on, if anyone mentioned church to me, I went. I wanted to hear more about Jesus.

And now, at the Aldermans almost two years after I had become a Christian, I was struggling with what to do with my life. Several people at church told me they knew exactly what that was: I was going to be a preacher.

During those months at the Aldermans, Norman and I spent many hours studying Scripture, including how to know God's will for my life. The decision about whether or not God was calling me to become a preacher weighed so heavily on my heart that finally one night as I sat in my bedroom I prayed, *"Lord, if this is what You want me to do, then let Norman tell me tonight where the qualifications for being a pastor are in the Bible."*

That was another fleece – one of dozens I've put out before the Lord over the years. Like Gideon in Judges 6, I wanted to be sure of God's will.

Then I told Carol about my prayer. At the very moment I was talking with her, Norman drove into the driveway. I went out to meet him and told him what was on my mind. He immediately told me to go inside and get my Bible. When I was seated, he sat in a chair directly in front of me, turned to 1 Timothy 3 and read the qualifications of a pastor: "If a man desires the office of a bishop, he desires a good work" (KJV). Norman kept on reading, but I didn't hear anything else because suddenly I felt something come over me. I knew what I would do with my life: The Lord was calling me to preach. I knew the Lord and I would walk closer than ever: I knew He would be more involved in my life than I had experienced before. There was no going back. The Lord had shown me without a doubt what He wanted me to do; I had to step into that role even though I didn't know what was involved. It was April 1973; I was seventeen and a half years old. I got my first experience preaching at Greenland Church as from time to time over the next year Norman let me preach.

WHILE THE ALDERMANS had made it clear that I could live with them as long as I wanted, at the beginning of summer 1973 the opportunity opened for me to live at Singing Hills Bible Camp in Corbin and serve as a junior counselor. I celebrated my eighteenth birthday there on July 31.

When summer ended, I had no place to live, so the camp's leaders invited me to live at the camp for my junior year. (By that time the

Aldermans were expecting their first child and even though I could have gone back to live with them, it would have been a tight squeeze.)

AS THE LORD continued to open new paths and opportunities, my personality began to change. I became more outgoing, I became more assertive, and I knew the weight for building a better life was no longer on my shoulders alone. Soon, anytime I felt God wanted me to do something, I did it. Whatever I went after, I achieved.

Before long I became a leader at school. I was elected vice president of the Whitley County High School's Future Farmers of America (FFA) club, president of the school's Christian Youth Club, and regional parliamentarian and state reporter for the Future Business Leaders of America (FBLA) – a role in which I served during my senior year. I became the first chaplain of the school's FFA chapter. I started reading the Bible over the school intercom each morning.

I also excelled in sports. I played basketball and ran track. I won my first-ever first place in anything in a two-mile race in Bowling Green, Kentucky.

And I got to travel. In fact, my first trip out of Whitley County was with the basketball team. Until then, I didn't even know other high schools existed. Through FFA, I went to the Kentucky State Fair in Louisville (three hours away) and attended a week-long state FFA leadership camp in Hardin County where I was one of two among the more than 200 campers who received an outstanding leadership award.

I took my first plane trip with FBLA when my state advisor and I flew to California for a national conference. I was so naïve that when we got near San Francisco I asked him where the cowboys and Indians were. He laughed and asked me why I was asking. I replied, "This is California, isn't it?" My image of the West came solely from television.

Looking back, it's almost hard to believe that just a few months before I'd felt there was nothing for me and if I disappeared, no one would even notice. Now, the Lord blessed everything I touched.

AS MY JUNIOR YEAR was coming to an end, once again I found I needed a place to live. By then, I'd learned to work and live in the moment, since I never knew how long I would be living at a given place before I would need to move to another. Looking back, the constant during this time was all my high school teachers were doing for me, no matter where I was living.

It was one of those teachers who took me in that June. Ed Teague, the never-married fifty-something head of the school's business department, and I had first become acquainted when I'd helped him with odd jobs on his farm. I lived with him through my senior year of high school and my first semester of college.

While I did work for him on his farm, it was only after I graduated from high school that I learned the extent of his financial investment in me. He not only provided my room and board but also paid for my books and my school lunches. He was proud of me when I graduated with honors in May 1975.

Mr. Teague became "Dad" to me. He helped me to build my character from the inside out. While I had changed much over the preceding years, I still had many rough edges, which Dad helped me smooth out. His friends were in a different social set than most of the people with whom I'd previously associated, so he introduced me to many new experiences. Dad and his friends regularly ate out in nice restaurants – something I'd never done. In contrast to most of the other people with whom I'd stayed, Dad was laid back. If I went to school, did my homework, and helped him around the farm, that was all he expected. It was an easy place to live.

As to how I began to call him "Dad" and he to call me "Son", it just happened. I do remember one hilarious incident that occurred shortly after I went to live with him. It seems that blackbirds had been eating Dad's corn so he borrowed a .22 rifle to take care of the problem. He then sent me into the store to buy shells. Problem was I was only nineteen and by law a person had to be twenty-one or have an adult sign in order to buy shells. When the store clerk asked if I had someone to sign, without thinking I immediately replied, "My dad's in the car and he can sign." I brought Dad in but didn't tell him what I had said. The clerk, who was a friend of Dad's, looked at me and at him and said, "Son, you're a lot taller than your dad is." I replied, "I guess I took after my mother." When we got back in the car, Dad laughed and laughed. "He (the clerk) thinks he's got something on me now," he said.

I would be remiss if I didn't add that for many years some in my biological family didn't understand why I had lived with Mr. Teague or why I called him "Dad" or even why I had stayed with so many families during my growing-up years. And, honestly, I didn't understand why they seemed to resent Dad and me so much. It was only around 2009 that I learned the full story. That year, I felt the Lord telling me it was time to talk it over with my brother David, who is two years older than I am. When I asked why my family had felt as they had about Dad and about how I'd lived my early years, David told me they'd thought I hadn't respected my upbringing and that I'd thought I was better than they were. He told me the incident that had brought it all to a head occurred when I'd been featured in a local newspaper article in which I'd called Mr. Teague "Dad." Plus, David said when I'd gone to live with the Aldermans after my mother and stepfather had abandoned me, my siblings thought pinto beans and cornbread weren't good enough for me. They'd thought I wanted steak.

I was blown away by what David said. For the first time in my life, I saw myself through the eyes of my biological family. As I talked with him, I think for the first time he saw me, too. I told him how I'd always felt that if our biological dad were alive he would be proud that someone like Dad had cared enough to look after his son. I told him Dad Teague not only had taken me in but also had been there for my wife and me at a crucial time in our lives (more about that in chapter three). I told him how Dad Teague had remained a very important person in my life until his death at age seventy-eight in 1994. Plus, I told David that while on occasion we did have steak at the Aldermans, pinto beans and cornbread were staples for them, too.

As David and I talked, it became clear to me that the true underlying reasons I'd lived with other people had never registered with any of my biological family. All they'd ever heard anyone say was that I had rejected them. I realized that in spite of all the time we'd been together as we were growing up we'd never really known each other. To me, it felt as if I'd just been visiting all those years. Plus, my family still didn't know what I'd accomplished in my adult life even though we lived in the same county. That day as David and I talked, it was like the coming together of two very different stories.

That day, I learned an important lesson that would stick with me to this day. I learned that to be able to build a relationship with someone, I first need to see a situation through the other person's eyes, not just my own. That day with David taught me to listen to the other person's version of his or her life story. It taught me that only then can a relationship have the potential to change and become healthy. Indeed, that day my relationship with David changed. David and I became brothers. An added bonus was that our conversation opened the door for me to talk with other family members.

Meantime, the Lord was preparing someone else to become an even more important person in my life. Her name was Joyce Davis.

---

LOOKING IN: *Norman and Carol Alderman*
*Keith had started coming to our church so I (Norm) visited in his home, talked with his mother, and saw the situation first-hand. Then, at some point, I remember sitting with Keith in my car, talking about his home life. It didn't take much to know that Keith was different from his family. He was a really good person; he exuded goodness.*

*When he came to prayer meeting that night in December 1972 and asked for a place to stay, Norm and I (Carol) felt so bad for him. At the time, we lived in a brand new 10 x 38 trailer with two small bedrooms, so we knew we had a bedroom for him. We talked it over and decided we should ask Keith to live with us.*

*And so we went to the Chambers' home where Keith was staying and invited him to our home. The invitation was open-ended; Keith could stay as long as he wished.*

*Looking back, we were reacting to what we believed to be the necessity of the moment. As it turned out, the timing was crucial because Keith was desperate.*

*It was a good match. During the time Keith lived with us, he was just a prince, so appreciative, so thoughtful. He never caused a minute's trouble. We didn't try to function as parents, partly because we were just a few years older than he; we were just friends.*

*Now, more than forty years later, as we look back Keith is a beautiful memory. Scripture says, "Cast your bread upon the waters: for thou shalt find it after many days" (Ecclesiastes 11:1, KJV). We helped him because he was a human being, he was a Christian boy, and he needed a place to live.*

Norman and Carol Alderman
Former pastor and wife, Greenland Baptist Church
Corbin, Kentucky
Living in Marlinton, West Virginia, in 2015

# Two

I may have been the answer to Joyce Davis' prayers but when we began dating and married four months later I don't think she knew what she was getting into. Actually, neither did I.

We had gotten together, thanks to the help of Joyce's mother. Unbeknownst to me, Joyce had had her eye on me for a long time. Even though we were in the same class at Whitley County High, I admit I hadn't noticed her. As Joyce tells the story, she'd known who I was since our freshman year. She knew that I had got saved/became a Christian, that I carried my Bible to school each day, and that I was speaking in churches around the county on many Sunday mornings. And of course, she heard me read the Bible each morning over the school intercom.

Me? "Keith didn't really pay any attention to me," Joyce says.

Plus, Joyce says she thought she wasn't good enough for me. She says she thought I deserved someone better. (How wrong she was!) Still, her heart turned toward me.

And then our June 1975 high school graduation came. That night, because Joyce's family name is Davis and mine is Decker we were seated side by side at the ceremony. Afterward, when Joyce saw me with another girl whom I'd been dating, she sat in her mom's car and cried. Wanting to help, Joyce's mother told her she was going right then and there to tell me about her daughter's feelings for me. Of course, Joyce was mortified and said, "No."

I must confess that after graduation, Joyce wasn't even on my radar screen as I preached and sang in churches around the area and prepared to begin classes at Cumberland College (now University of the Cumberlands) in Williamsburg that fall. Then in November my sister Kathy asked me to help out at White Oak Baptist Church where she had visited. Now, White Oak was Joyce's parents' church and they were key leaders there. One Sunday morning Joyce's mom invited me to go home with her for Sunday dinner, and then – unbeknownst to her – Joyce's dad invited me, too. I readily accepted. Imagine Joyce's surprise when she came home from her church to find me at her table!

From then on, every time I visited in the Davis home, Joyce's mother went to great lengths to make sure Joyce and I had time alone. I remember one occasion when her mom even asked me to give Joyce a ride to a Sunday night service at White Oak Church just to put us together for a few minutes, I think. (I admit I still wasn't interested in Joyce.) Looking back, Joyce remembers her mom saying, "If those two are going to get together, they're going to need some help" – and she was glad to give it.

Finally, I did get interested in Joyce and gained enough confidence to ask her to go to a movie. Then in December we drove six miles to Cumberland Falls for our official first date. From then on, all our dates were spent in church. We never did get officially engaged; it was just understood that someday we would marry.

Meanwhile, I was busy with my studies to become a Certified Public Accountant. (I planned to be a bi-vocational pastor, as well.) As part of my college curriculum, I worked part-time at Rose Bookkeeping Service in Corbin. By then, I'd moved from Dad Teague's home and was living with my Aunt Ruby Bryant. That move had really hurt Dad Teague. He just couldn't understand why I wanted to leave. As has happened so often over the subsequent years, I had only one answer: The Lord had told me to move, and I had obeyed. It took a while for Dad Teague to begin to understand. Actually, when he met Joyce the ice broke and he began to see how God was working in my life. I lived with Aunt Ruby for a few weeks, and then my brother Woodrow and I rented a trailer together.

JOYCE AND I continued to date during that December, but until that point I hadn't thought about marriage. I'd thought of Joyce as a very special person whom I enjoyed being with, and I loved the fact that she loved the Lord and was a joy to be around.

That changed when one day as I was driving to work I felt the Lord asking me to pray concerning whether to marry Joyce. *"If the light is on in my office when I arrive at work, then Joyce and I aren't to get married. If, however, the light is not on, we are to get married,"* I was led to pray.

The result? The light was on; I wasn't to marry Joyce, which tore me up emotionally all day. I simply couldn't imagine Joyce and me just being friends – but even worse than that, I couldn't imagine not doing God's will. After we'd started dating, I hadn't missed a single day going to her house to visit her, but that night I just couldn't bring myself to go. I was in turmoil.

Later that night, I resigned myself to the fact that Joyce and I were not to marry. *"Okay, Lord, if that's what You want, that's what I'll do,"* I prayed.

The next morning, however, when I was driving at the very same spot where I'd been the day before when I'd felt led to pray, the Lord asked me to pray again. I said, *"No,"* because I didn't want the previous message verified.

Then the Lord said something He knew would cause me to pray again. He said, *"Are you afraid?"*

At that question, I prayed the same prayer as the day before. As I pulled into the parking lot and looked at my window, my heart dropped: There was a light. I went to my office with a heavy heart, but then I saw something wonderful: The light shining in my office was not from an electrical bulb, but it was a ray of light from the sky! I was to marry Joyce! I knelt in that light and said, *"Thank you, Lord."*

After work, I picked Joyce up at her house and we went out to talk. I asked her to pray about whether we should get married. She replied that she was also putting out a fleece: If her dad was at home when we got back, then we were to marry. When we got home, he was sitting in his chair!

Later, I understood that what God was doing was testing me to see who I would choose to be number one in my life – Him or Joyce. I'd chosen Him. And He blessed me with Joyce.

At first, Joyce and I said we would wait to get married until I had finished college. Then we said we would wait until the end of the spring semester. Then Christmas Eve 1975 came.

That Christmas Eve night Joyce and I were attending a service at our church when the Spirit of the Lord just took over. All of a sudden, people were falling out of their seats, and kids were rising out of the pews and falling over. Some people thought the cause was carbon monoxide from the floor furnace, so someone called Emergency Medical Services to take all of us to the local hospital emergency room. We were examined and sent home; there was no evidence of carbon monoxide.

Interestingly, as Joyce and I were riding with my brother back to the church, his car quit running. He left the car to go across the road to find a phone to call for help. That left Joyce and me in the back seat. For the first time, I realized if something happened to Joyce, I would be traumatized. The Spirit of the Lord was working in me, too. I knew the Lord meant for us to marry soon.

Three months later on March 06, 1976, we were married by Norman Alderman at Greenland Baptist Church. Dad Teague came to our wedding, which thrilled me. The day before, on March 05, I had been ordained to the gospel ministry at White Oak Baptist Church. (I wrote about my call to ministry in chapter one.) Even though Joyce and I never talked about our plans for the future, we were secure in knowing that more than anything we wanted to follow the Lord.

After we married, we moved into a rental house in Corbin and lived there for a couple of months. Then we moved into a trailer/mobile home near Joyce's mom and dad's home in Williamsburg.

IN THE FIRST years after I graduated from high school, many life-changing events happened. Each affected me in its own way. Those years are best told chronologically.

In *September 1975*, a few months before Joyce and I married, my stepdad, Steve Love, died, which set me on a journey to dig into my past. I began thinking about what I'd been told about how my biological dad had given me away when I was a baby. I wanted to confirm what I'd heard about how a doctor had told Gladys Mullis – the nurse who had taken me in – that I wouldn't live. So when I went for a physical exam, I asked my doctor about it. When he looked at the x-ray of my lungs, he confirmed I had suffered from pneumonia when I was very young. I could rest assured the story was true: I'd been very ill and at the point of death when I was a baby.

That made me determined to find Gladys, so I learned where she and her husband lived and went to see them. Her husband answered my knock on the door and I asked to see Gladys. When she came to the door, I said, "I'm Keith Decker." She just stood there for a while, going back in time in her mind. Then she grabbed me, hugged me, and told her husband, "This is our baby." She phoned her daughters and they came over. They told me I had been like a brother to them, as we hugged and reminisced.

It was awesome. From that day until Gladys died, the Lord intertwined our walkings. One vivid example came when I'd been involved in a car accident and was in the hospital. Joyce was concerned about leaving me alone when she had to go to her job. Then, from the other side of the pulled divider curtain, we heard words we will never forget: "Don't worry. I took care of him when he was a baby, and I'll take care of him now." It was Gladys. She'd been hired to care for an elderly minister who was in the bed next to me. Until Gladys' death, Joyce and I took her to church with us most Sundays and spent a lot of time with her most weeks.

In *early 1976* shortly after Joyce and I married, I dropped out of college. When I had entered Cumberland College in the fall of 1975, I'd assumed that the next step in following the Lord was for me to complete four years and graduate, but then the Lord intervened and told me to drop out. That's one of the hardest things I've ever done. As I considered it, I realized how many people had invested in me and how they would be disappointed. I prayed hard about the decision.

*"Lord, surely You don't want me to quit after I've come this far. How can I face all the people who have helped me?"* I prayed.

Still, I knew beyond a doubt the Lord was telling me to quit; I knew I had to do what He said. In a cowardly moment, I decided I would simply not show up for classes anymore, but then the Lord clearly told me I had to tell my professors in person. I especially dreaded telling my religion professor until I remembered one of the main things he had stressed that semester was that we should trust God even when we don't know what He is doing. I also dreaded going to the dean of men, too, but when he asked me why I was dropping out and I told him that the Lord had told me to, he told me there was no better reason.

And so I dropped out in the middle of the second semester of my freshman year. For the record, a few years later I did return to Cumberland College and completed two additional years in accounting. Should I ever return to college, I would study religion.

In *April,* one month after Joyce and I married, I was laid off by the bookkeeping firm where I was working because the job had been a part of my college studies and I was no longer in school. A week later, I found a job as payroll clerk at T.C. Young Construction.

In *May,* Joyce got pregnant. We were very happy because we both wanted a family. Sadly, in *September* there were complications with the pregnancy and I had to make the gut-wrenching decision between saving Joyce's life and saving our baby's life. Dad Teague was with me when I got that news and gave me some wise advice: "You can always have more children, but there's only one Joyce," he said. It would be fifteen years before children would grace our home.

In *December,* Joyce quit the job at American Greetings that she'd had since graduating from high school. Losing our baby had taken a toll on her.

In *May 1977,* I learned I had an illness that I would have to deal with for the rest of my life. It began innocently enough. By that time I was working as payroll clerk for C. and C. Contracting Company in Williamsburg, which was run by the daughter of my previous boss, T.C. Young at T.C. Young Construction. One day as I was running an errand for the company, I pulled a muscle in my back as I got out of the car. The pain was so bad that I was barely able to make it to my doctor's office a few blocks away. As was the custom, the doctor called a local funeral home to send a hearse to transport me to the hospital. Joyce still vividly remembers someone from Vankirk Funeral Home calling and saying, "This is Vankirk Funeral Home," then pausing before asking her to go to Corbin Hospital. She was scared to death.

I was in the hospital for a week, during which time I was given heavy pain medication for my constant pain, which only made matters worse. Finally, I was sent to a hospital in Lexington, a hundred miles away. There, a doctor hooked me up to an IV and told a nurse to let me dry out; he thought I was a drug addict. (To that time, I'd never been sick in my adult life; the strongest medication I'd ever taken was aspirin. I ran and exercised regularly and was in great physical condition.) So for three days, I got IVs only. The next thing I remember is a lot of medical personnel gathered around me and a tongue depressor hanging over my bed. I had no idea what it was used for until a nurse told me I'd had a seizure. When I asked my roommate what had happened, he told me when I'd gotten out of bed and into the bathroom, I'd passed out.

I was diagnosed with epilepsy.

Looking back, Joyce says she'd noticed something was wrong within the first couple of weeks of our marriage as I would have small seizures which didn't last too long, but she had never said anything about it. Also, she says that Dad Teague had mentioned one episode that had happened in my senior year when I was working on his farm and couldn't figure out how to complete a simple task. Dad Teague had taken me to the doctor, but since I had no symptoms nothing had come of it.

In college, I'd experienced one episode, but it hadn't been diagnosed as epilepsy. That day as I was taking a zoology exam, I found myself stalled on one question; I simply couldn't move on to answer any more questions.

Now in *May 1977*, there was no doubt: I had epilepsy. After I got home from the hospital in Lexington I was able to return to work and continue driving until I had an automobile accident as I was driving Joyce and another woman to work at the American Greetings plant in Corbin. (By then, Joyce had returned to work.) Neither the woman nor I was hurt in the accident, but Joyce had a broken collarbone. The police took my driver's license, which meant that because Joyce didn't have a driver's license she had to learn to drive. She drove me to work every day for the next two years.

Plus, when Joyce was taking a physical exam connected with the accident, we learned she was pregnant again, which made us very happy. Everything seemed fine with this pregnancy.

In *August 1977*, I quit my job over some issues that were important to me. A few days after I quit, an extraordinary opportunity presented itself. As I was walking down the street in Williamsburg, I came upon Williamsburg Ford, a major automobile dealership in the area. Immediately I felt the Lord telling me to walk in and ask about getting a job there. Now, picture this: I was dressed in overalls, a work shirt, and boots – not exactly clothes for an unplanned interview at a successful business. When the owner asked about my job skills, I told him I'd worked as a payroll clerk in an office. He hired me on the spot to do the follow-up paperwork to sales deals and to make bank deposits. I was on salary and was in line to have my own brand-new car after six months on the job. I was twenty-two years old.

In *September 1997*, I quit my job. While the work came easy for me, as a newly-wed the long hours were hard on my family life. When I talked with the owner – who was a dedicated Christian – about the fact that I didn't have a life outside work, he wrote out an agreement stating I had the freedom to take time off anytime any day I needed to. The only requirement was that I get all my work done. I should have seen it as the perfect job.

In the meantime, however, many well-meaning Christian friends were telling me I was wasting my life at the dealership. They thought because

I was working such long hours for little pay the dealership was just using me. And so I quit. Big mistake. I learned some big lessons then, two of which are "Don't tell anybody how much money you make" and "Don't ever tell anybody everything you're thinking." As Scripture says, "Don't let the left hand know what the right hand is doing" (my paraphrase of Matthew 6:3, KJV).

Looking back, I have to ask myself, *"Why in the world would you leave a place like that?"* At the time, it didn't dawn on me what I was doing. I now know I took my eyes off the Lord instead of staying focused on the fact that He had helped me get the job. I forgot to ask the Lord what He wanted me to do; instead I listened to other people. Unlike other times when I'd listened for the voice of God and He had guided me, this time, I didn't listen and He chastised me. Plus, I let down people who believed in me, and it took a long time to rebuild their trust. And I no longer had a job.

In *September 1977*, tragedy hit once again. We lost our second son, Keith Edward Decker, Jr., at five and a half months. We learned Joyce had some of the same problems carrying a baby to term that her mother had experienced. Her mom had lost three babies, all born prematurely. Her mother had always called Joyce her miracle baby. In the midst of our sorrow, God gave me a word of hope at our son's funeral: He told me that someday Joyce would carry a baby to term.

By *December 1977*, our financial resources were running low, to say the least. Joyce and I have never been ones to ask for help or to let anyone know our financial situation, but somehow a local church learned about our need and took up an offering for us. We loved those people and the pastor, but after they presented us with the money in a worship service we felt we could never go back there. We wondered if the people would ever look at us the same again. We wondered if they would just see us as people who took handouts.

When people did begin to learn about our dwindling resources, many encouraged us to sign up for food stamps. Finally we did, but after our first trip to the grocery with food stamps we decided we couldn't use them. There we were wearing our good go-to-work clothes, taking a handout. We could feel people looking at us. Joyce and I agreed we should give the remaining stamps back and just trust the Lord. And we did. We both were concerned about our Christian testimony. We believed that God would supply our needs.

In those first years of our marriage, God often used Joyce's Mom and Dad and Dad Teague to help us, even when we didn't tell them we were in need. Dad Teague always gave us money for birthdays, Christmas, and other special events. Other people also helped us from time to time.

THEN CAME Christmas 1979. We had nothing under the tree. Plus, Joyce was sick. As we sat at home, there came a knock at our trailer door. A couple came in and gave us a Christmas gift – a candy dish – which was strange since we hadn't told anyone about how bad our financial situation had gotten. After they left, I went into our bedroom – which was also my prayer room – and lay down on my face and prayed.

*"Lord,"* I begged, *"I need Your help tonight."*

When I went back into the living room, I just sat down and watched the clock. At about 8 o'clock, I saw car lights coming down our driveway. Then I saw more car lights behind the first. It looked like an entire church congregation had come.

By the time those people left, the space under our tree was full of gifts, our table was full of gifts, our cabinets were full of food, and we had a $300 check to boot. The good folk at Sandstone Baptist Church in Corbin blessed us that night. It seems the couple who had brought us the candy dish had gone back to the church and told the people about our situation and the people had gathered up gifts for us. The gifts they brought had names that had been crossed out and our names put in their places – they had given us their gifts. When Joyce and I saw that, it was almost as much a blessing as the gifts themselves.

Looking back, from the beginning of our marriage Joyce and I have always known God will help us when the need arises. We also have always known we are not to take anything that will move us away from our closeness with Him. Looking back at those hard times, we know God was molding us for what lay ahead.

FOR THREE YEARS after I was diagnosed with epilepsy, most of the time I couldn't drive or work. I couldn't provide a regular income for Joyce and me. Often I couldn't even figure out how to get from our trailer to my workshop in the back yard. In reality, I couldn't do much of anything. It was humiliating; it worked on my mind. Those years tried my very soul.

Before my diagnosis, I'd helped out as a lay leader at Black Oak Baptist Church on the Kentucky-Tennessee border. I wanted so much to continue, but the epilepsy put that in doubt. Often, I'd sit in my car for hours wondering whether I should go to church, or I'd sit by our front door and wait from morning until evening for Joyce to come home from work. Joyce always drove me to church for services but without my driver's license I couldn't drive to visit people in the church community. Sometimes I was so determined that I would hitchhike to do my visiting. Several times I thought I was clear of episodes and would be able to get my license back, but then I'd have an episode that would knock me back and I would have to start all over again. (At the time, Kentucky law required that a person be free of epileptic episodes for one year before a driver's license could be reinstated.)

The worst trial for me was that Joyce had to become the sole breadwinner for our family. By that time she had taken a job at Hillcrest Nursing Home in Corbin, so we lived on her income and my disability check. Never in my adult life had anybody had to pay my bills. I tried my best to help out by taking odd jobs when my health permitted, but it just wasn't the same as bringing in a regular paycheck. Soon we were in dire financial straits.

Another sorrow entered our home as well when Joyce's mom, Arley Mae Hickey Davis, got cancer. We brought her to live with us and to care for her. One blessing came in that because I wasn't working, I was able to help take care of her. She died on Oct. 08, 1980.

FOR THREE YEARS, dealing with epilepsy was the focus of our lives. While my epilepsy had been diagnosed a few months before I quit my brief job at Williamsburg Ford, I know beyond a doubt that the severity of the disease was a direct chastisement from God for giving up that job. Quitting was a stupid thing to do because He didn't tell me to quit. (I must admit over the next years after I quit there were times when the devil tried to make me believe God wasn't just chastising me but was punishing me. I never gave in to the devil's false teaching.)

I'm often asked why I believe epilepsy was God's chastisement on me and what I believe to be the difference between God's chastisement, punishment, and trials. Here's how I see it: Hebrews 12:6 says "for whom the Lord loveth he chastens" (KJV). Chastisement is a whipping to bring us back in line and thus to avoid God's punishment, which brings His judgment. To understand this, we have only to look at His treatment of the children of Israel. When they first rebelled against His plans for them, God put them through chastisings/whippings to bring them back to Himself. When they continued to rebel, they faced God's severe punishment/ judgment. As for trials, we have only to look at Job. God wasn't chastising him nor was He punishing him because Job hadn't done anything wrong. Instead, God allowed bad things to happen to Job in order to bring out a better Job.

The lesson is that first God chastises His children to bring them back in line. God chastises us in order to bring us back to Himself and help us determine never, ever to fail Him in that way again. If we change, then chastisement keeps punishment from happening; if we don't listen and change our ways, then He punishes us. God's punishment comes when we have knowingly done something contrary to His law and have refused to change. The degree of His punishment is dependent on how many times He has to tell us to repent and change our ways.

As for trials, they come when we are doing the right things and God wants to refine us so we will do even greater things for His glory. At the end of every trial is a blessing if we will stay the course and let God do His work in us. In fact, the size of the blessing is in direct proportion to the size of the trial. Scripture promises "the trying of faith works patience. But let patience have her perfect work, that ye may be perfect and entire, wanting nothing" (James 1:3-4, KJV). This is the meaning of the doctrine of sanctification, the process of putting off the old self and putting on the new self and becoming like Christ (Ephesians 4:22-24).

As for me, when I left Williamsburg Ford I listened to the voice of people instead of the voice of God. Looking back, God had already invested much in me and in my future; through the years He had provided places for me to live and people to help prepare me to have a productive, God-centered life. By then, I'd already come to see each place I'd lived as a training camp for who He wanted me to be: At one place I learned grammar; at another, good manners; at another, how to dress properly – Dad Teague would never let me leave home without shining my shoes: at another, how to present myself in public; and on and on the list went. Somehow I forgot all the ways God had cared for me. Most importantly, I forgot the way He had taught me to make life decisions: I was to wait for a specific word from Him, not a word from any human being.

Looking back, leaving that job made it harder for God to get me to where He wanted me to be. Because my boss was a strong Christian and created a Christian environment at Williamsburg Ford, I know had I stayed I would have been nurtured as a believer. I simply didn't realize what I had – and I walked away.

For the apostle Paul, it took three days of chastisement (Acts 9:9); for me, it took three years. I learned when you listen to other people instead of listening to the Lord, it takes longer to get to where He wants you to be. It's like you have to circle back to where you once were before you can move forward.

AFTER THREE LONG years, at long last the epilepsy was under control enough so that I could look for a full-time job. Excited about the possibility of returning to work, I took refresher courses in typing and bookkeeping through a government retraining program to get me back on track. I wanted to be ready to apply for a job at Appalachian Computer Services (ACS) in London, about thirty miles north of Williamsburg. The medicine I'd been taking for the epilepsy had caused my hands to draw inward, so learning to type again was an uphill battle. The test at ACS required typing fifty-five words a minute with no more than five mistakes. I worked and worked but could only get to forty words. I decided to take the test anyway. Joyce and I prayed and prayed.

When I took the one-minute test, I knew immediately that I hadn't passed. The teacher asked me if I wanted to come back to take the two-minute test, implying there was no need to try it. I said, "Yes."

For the two-minute test, I prayed even more. *"Lord,"* I prayed, *"You've given me the opportunity; now give me the ability."*

When the time for the two-minute test came and I put my fingers on the computer keyboard, I was amazed as I watched them. They were moving so fast.

After I'd finished the test, the person giving the test told me that I'd typed seventy-five words per minute with five mistakes on the two tests combined! That meant on the second test I'd typed more than one hundred words a minute.

I started work at ACS on the Monday after I took the test. I began work in data entry and later was promoted to data processor and then to audit analyst. The company also paid for me to return to college. I worked there for nine years. Joyce also worked for ACS from 1984 to 1990.

The Lord also opened the door for me to fulfill the call I had felt at age seventeen while I was living with the Aldermans: I become a pastor. One day as I was working in our back yard a man from First Baptist Church in Rockholds about ten miles south of Corbin called to ask if I would preach at the church. When Joyce told me what he wanted, the Spirit of the Lord leaped in my heart and I knew my chastisement was over. Later, as Joyce and I talked about what I'd felt when the man called, we both felt we were like Mary, the mother of Jesus, who pondered things in her heart until she understood what they meant. One thing Joyce and I knew for sure: God had let us know that my chastisement was over. (The epilepsy would not be under control until October 1995 when the correct medications and dosage were finally found. Epilepsy, however, would be a serious part of my life for the rest of my life.)

I became pastor at Rockholds on July 08, 1984, and stayed there for five years. When I became pastor, I was almost twenty-nine years old.

The following year, 1985, also held much sorrow for Joyce and me. Her father, Jim Franklin Davis, died on April 13. My mother, Hettie Mable Walters Hensley Decker Love, died on Oct. 03.

LOOKING BACK, had I not gone through those hard years, I could not have become an effective pastor. From the time I was called to preach, I'd always felt the Lord was calling me to help churches that were experiencing problems. Had I not gone through the Lord's chastisement, I know I would have given up at the sign of the first church fight.

During those years the Lord taught me that with every chastisement comes a blessing, and the harder the chastisement, the bigger the blessing. If I hadn't gone through the chastisement of epilepsy, I wouldn't be the person I am today. During those years, people often asked me if I was still preaching or if I had given that up. During those years of chastisement, I often asked myself, *"Why this? Have I done something so wrong that the Lord has to keep on chastising me for so long?"*

But during those years I also learned we aren't born with staying power; it has to be created in us by the Lord. Looking back, I know it was only by His grace that I didn't give up.

Little did I know how much I would need staying power over the following years nor how quickly the Lord's grace would direct my life onto a new, unexpected path. This time, I would trust and obey.

# Three

In 1990, Joyce and I decided she should quit work and focus on starting a family. By then, we'd been married for fourteen years and were beginning to doubt we would ever have biological children in spite of the Lord's promise to me when our second son had died that Joyce would carry a child to term. In the meantime, as we prayed we heard the Lord telling us to become foster parents.

That year as we prepared, we learned we would need at least six families to take the required course for becoming foster parents. True to the nature of the people at Corn Creek Baptist Church where I was now pastor, four other families from the church gladly took the course. With another couple from the area and Joyce and me, that made the required six. (By that time, Joyce and I had moved from our trailer into her parents' home, which we'd bought after their deaths.)

In January 1991, our first foster child came to live with us for about a month. He was seventeen and almost blind. He came with long hair, earrings, guns and roses tattoos, and a butcher knife. He was tough. Things changed when I told him about my life growing up – he said he guessed he didn't need his butcher knife after all. One day when he asked me to get him a couple of cigarettes, I made a deal with him: If he'd get a haircut and put on good clothes for his upcoming required visit to Social Services, then I'd give him the cigarettes. He responded, "Good Lord, all that for a couple of cigarettes." He did what I'd asked. He looked so different that when we met his case worker she didn't recognize him. True to my word, I bought him the cigarettes.

Then in March 1991, two boys, ages ten and eleven, came. One stayed with us for two years. The other, Terry, stayed until he turned eighteen.

(In 2015, Terry and his wife, Summer, live in Tennessee with their two children, Braeden and Gracyn Maggie. A truck driver, he stops in to visit us from time to time. He loves Mom Joyce's cooking. He – and Summer – especially love her banana pudding.)

Seven months after the two boys came, a thirteen-month-old girl named Renee Joy came to live with us. Three years later, we began the adoption process for Renee, thinking she would complete our family. (In 2015, Renee Joy and her husband, Christopher Miracle, and their two children, Destiney and Dalton, live a few miles away from us.)

But the Lord had other plans. In early 1994, Joyce got pregnant. Admittedly, that was a big surprise since by that time we'd been married seventeen years. Interestingly, even before Joyce knew she was pregnant, I told her she was – to which she replied, "You're crazy." So I sent her to the doctor to check it out. Sure enough, when she returned she said she was pregnant. "You never gave up, did you?" she told me. This was, and is today, the relationship we have with each other and with the Lord.

During the pregnancy Joyce had only one frightening incident, which occurred at the exact same time in the pregnancy as when we had lost our first two babies. When she started bleeding badly, I took her to the hospital – and I called the members of Corn Creek Baptist Church to prayer. Our prayers were answered: The doctor said everything was fine.

At last the time came for the birth – or so we thought. We made the trip to the University of Kentucky Hospital in Lexington only to have the doctors send Joyce back home. Meanwhile, Dad Teague was taken to Central Baptist Hospital in Lexington, a few blocks away from UK Hospital. Unfortunately, when I visited him there, I didn't realize how serious the situation was – he was dying. He died on Nov. 25, 1994.

A few days later, Joyce, Renee, and I returned to UK Hospital. Now it was time. Holly Angel "Holly" Decker was born on Dec. 01, 1994. God had kept the promise He had made to me when our second son had died.

I was with Joyce when she gave birth to Holly but had to leave immediately to go back to Corbin to take Renee to stay with a friend, Imogene Frechette. Plus, I had to preach at Corn Creek Church. During that service, my epilepsy returned. Thankfully, Imogene's daughter, Mary, and Mary's husband, Doyle Hurst, drove me back to Lexington to pick up Joyce and Holly and bring them home.

Joyce has always believed that the death of Dad Teague – the man who had raised me from the time I was seventeen and had paid my way through high school and had become a father to me – was a major cause for the return of epilepsy. I think it was his death coupled with my concern for Joyce and the safe arrival of our baby. Yes, the burdens were heavy. Looking back, with the safe arrival of Holly I experienced one of the greatest joys of my life, but at the same time with the death of Dad just a week before, I experienced one of the worst. Plus, after Holly's birth, I was concerned for Joyce's health.

BACK TO 1991. Everything seemed to be on track in the Decker household. Joyce was happy being a stay-at-home mom with our foster children. I was doing well in my job at Appalachian Computer Services. I was in my third year as pastor of Corn Creek Baptist Church in Woodbine, and I was taking college classes.

Then the shoe dropped. After nine years with ACS, my job was eliminated and I was laid off. To be truthful, I thought the layoff was temporary – and I knew how I wanted to spend the down time. For several years, I'd been thinking about being full-time in the Lord's work, but I'd never known exactly what I was supposed to do. Now I thought that while I was receiving severance pay for nine weeks, just maybe the Lord would show me what to do.

Three days after I was laid off, the whole thing blew wide open. From that point in September 1991 until the present day, I've known beyond a shadow of a doubt what God wants me to do with my life.

---

LOOKING IN: *Joyce Decker*
*With the arrival of Terry, Renee, and Holly, our family was complete. God had given me the desires of my heart. My dream to marry a godly man and to have children had come true.*

Joyce Decker
Cedaridge Ministries

# Four

Y ou could say that my life's work began with a pile of left-over rummage sale items. Sometime in that eventful year of 1991, Janus Jones, the director of missions for Mt. Zion Baptist Association of Southern Baptist churches in Whitley County, had asked if I would serve as the volunteer youth director of the association. I agreed, and the association's youth leadership committee and I quickly organized Saturday night youth rallies that met at local Baptist churches. Attendance at the meetings grew rapidly from about 100 to 400, and meetings went from being quarterly to monthly. The rallies featured the youth themselves providing skits, music, and whatever else they wanted to do. Most importantly, about fifty youth were saved/professed faith in Jesus as Savior in the first year.

Because we primarily focused on the many smaller churches in the association that couldn't sustain youth programs by themselves, the space in the churches where we met was often maxed out. I remember one month when we were scheduled to meet at Corn Creek Baptist where I was pastor but I knew our sanctuary couldn't hold all the youth who would come. What to do? I took out all the pews so we could squeeze in a few more people. It wasn't long, however, before even such drastic actions didn't help; we'd outgrown the facilities of all our participating churches. Again, what to do? The youth leadership committee and I began to talk about buying the empty Rockholds School building for our very own youth center.

We knew we'd need to raise all the money needed for such a project, so we tried everything we could imagine. When Janus suggested that we ask churches in Mt. Zion Association to come together for a gigantic yard sale, the youth leadership committee eagerly bought into the idea. We were thrilled when forty churches signed up and a local business paid the rent for the Williamsburg Convention and Tourism Center in which to hold the sale. We hoped that by the end of that November day we'd have made enough money to be well on our way to buying the school; instead, when we tallied our receipts, we had netted only $400 – and we had loads of items left over.

Then I had the bright idea of storing the items in the basement of the associational office. Funny thing, Janus had been tickled to death when we'd cleaned out the basement of left-over items from a previous yard sale he'd held. Now that we were returning with even more items, well, that wasn't any fun. All I could think to do was move the stuff from the basement to the parking lot each day and try to sell it. On the first day, when three or four volunteers came to help we soon realized we had a cash register but no cash for change, so we pooled our spare change – all of $20. We were in business.

Imagine my and Janus' surprise when within a few days the parking lot was filled with even more items that people had dropped off. As for the basement, it had become so crammed that every morning it took me two hours to move enough stuff to the parking lot to make room just to walk about inside. Then every evening it took me two more hours to put it back. In fact, at night in order to lock the door, I had to crawl over all the stuff and then crawl back to get to the stairs to get out.

According to Janus, that was just one of many amusing sights during those months. He likes to tell how I bought two truckloads of bicycles to sell on the parking lot. He says he thought there was no way I could sell them, but I did. Laughingly, Janus says I convinced people they needed bicycles.

Janus' favorite story, however, is about the day I got my Bronco and trailer stuck on the hill behind the association's office. I regularly used the vehicle to pick up items people gave me for the rummage sales, and that day the trailer and Bronco were filled to capacity. When I saw police officers coming toward me, I naturally thought they were coming to help pull me out. Not so. Unbeknownst to me, that morning the bank on the corner had been robbed. Of course, the officers thought I was the robber, especially since for some reason I was wearing a ridiculous white lab coat. Janus looked out his office window and saw me with my hands on top of my car, feet spread like a criminal. He laughed and laughed. I didn't think it was so funny at the time.

Over the next months, the youth leaders, the youth, and I tried everything we could think of to raise money. We participated in community carnivals, selling food and drinks and managing game booths. We held aluminum can drives, collecting the cans to sell to recycling facilities. The money we raised, however, was just a drop in the bucket of what we needed to buy the school. So we rented the school building for several months until the building was taken off the market. That put us back to square one, which was just where God wanted us.

NONE OF US had any idea what God was about to do. I certainly didn't know He was redirecting my life. Looking back, Janus agrees. What developed was a "God-thing," he says. "It was not in anybody's mind."

By February 1992, it had become obvious that we needed a place for more than just yard sales; we needed space in which to operate a thrift store. So that month we incorporated as a non-profit 501(c) (3) with a governing board of directors and I was named president.

That spring, we rented a storefront on Main Street in Williamsburg and opened the thrift store. Baptist youth as well as adult volunteers from local churches helped me run it.

Within two months, we'd outgrown the Main Street space and were faced with yet another decision about our future. When I found a storefront on Third Street that was three times the size of the Main Street store, I approached the board of directors with the possibility of moving. As I've always done over the years since, I asked the board to put out a fleece before the Lord to see what He would have us do. All the board members agreed to the fleece, which was that if the woman who owned the building would give us one month's rent free ($200) and $50 in cash to buy paint for the space, we would move.

With the board members sitting before me, I called the woman to make our offer. At first she said she would give us the first month's free rent but not the $50 because she hadn't yet received a dime from us. And so I told her, "Sis, I can tell you if you agree to the deal, we will always pay our rent. If you don't agree, that's okay." She said she'd give us the $50. The deal was sealed. Sadly, even though all the board members had agreed to putting out that specific fleece, some of them resigned from the board or just quit coming to meetings after that.

Looking back, I know it was the Lord's doing that day. We had asked Him to show us what to do and He did. He opened that door.

We moved to Third Street under a lease/purchase agreement. By then, it had become evident the effort was no longer going to be a fund-raiser for the associational youth program nor was it going to be just a thrift store. What had begun with a pile of left-over rummage-sale items had become a ministry in and of itself. Plus, inasmuch as the school building we had hoped to buy for a youth center was no longer available, we didn't need to raise funds for the project. After many intense discussions with Mt. Zion Association's leadership, we came to a mutual agreement that the ministry would no longer be under the umbrella of the association. We agreed it had grown beyond being a fund-raiser for the association's youth program and was becoming a much broader-based ministry. We agreed the $5,000 we'd raised would stay with Mt. Zion Baptist Association.

From that time, the ministry has been an entity separate from Mt. Zion association. Janus Jones says that while the association "was never formally the sponsor of [what later became known as] Cedaridge," the association "did provide some leadership with organization papers, constitution, and by-laws." Janus also served on the board of directors for several years, volunteered in the thrift store, and helped me with several projects.

By then, I also knew God was calling me to serve the poor and needy of our community as well as be a pastor of a church. Now the ministry was solely dedicated to that purpose. I also knew I wouldn't be looking for secular employment again.

That began a journey with my Lord that I could never have dreamed up. With no training or experience in social work or the helping professions, I was to learn more about trusting God to meet the needs of hurting people than I ever thought possible. I quickly learned the Lord would use my growing-up experiences to help me minister to those in need. Having gone without food, having been homeless, and having lived from pillar to post gave me an understanding of needy people I couldn't have gotten any other way. I could easily picture a family as they received a bag of potatoes or a box of food that would ease their hunger. I could easily picture a father or mother planting the seed potatoes they'd received, and I could easily pray with them that the harvest would be good. I could easily put myself in the shoes of most of the people helped through our ministry.

I came to believe the Lord had allowed me to be homeless and hungry as preparation for my life's work. I'd grown up with practically nothing, and now I was starting a ministry from nothing to help people who, too, had practically nothing.

Looking back, my call to minister to the needy was a progression: God brought me from being a person in need to the place where He showed me people in need before He actually showed me how to meet their needs. By that time, He had given me the compassion, desire, and some know-how to meet those needs. All I had to do was to wait for God to put the connections together. And He did.

AS WE SET OUT on a new path, the board of directors and I didn't want to duplicate what other area ministries were doing. Instead, we wanted to come alongside them and offer whatever help we could. In order to determine our ministry niche, we convened a meeting of leaders of other helping agencies in the community to get their input. Together we determined that because no other ministry in the area could handle multiple large shipments, we would take that on as our ministry niche. We felt we could best serve by becoming a distribution center, not primarily a direct-help ministry. We, however, would continue to provide a direct-help thrift store.

As for the name, sometime along the way Cedaridge Ministries was chosen. Honestly, I'm not sure exactly how or when or why. Looking back, the only thing I can think of is that the name Cedaridge is a combination of the names of two favorite Southern Baptist retreat centers: the Kentucky Baptist Convention's Cedarmore Assembly in Bagdad, Kentucky; and the Southern Baptist Convention's Ridgecrest Conference Center near Asheville, North Carolina.

SOON AFTER WE moved to Third Street, the Lord confirmed the ministry's niche in a big way. One day as I waited in line at another ministry in town to pick up bales of clothing for our thrift shop, I overheard a truck driver talking about how he had delivered a semi-load of food to another ministry that had distributed half the load and let the other half spoil. I immediately replied out of my spirit, "Brother, I guarantee if I'm given a semi-load of food, I won't let it spoil even if I have to distribute all of it myself." The man then asked me when I wanted some food to be delivered. I replied, "Tomorrow."

Imagine my shock the next day when a semi backed up to our door with 900 forty-five pound boxes of bananas. That's about twenty tons. You need to remember this was downtown Williamsburg and there was no place to park a semi and we had no loading dock. Quickly, I began pulling people off the street and offering them bananas if they would help deliver bananas to people who needed them. And they did. Within six hours, we had delivered all the bananas to needy individuals and to local ministries and churches we knew would give them to needy people.

That load of bananas was our first large shipment. That day, I knew the Lord had confirmed Cedaridge's mission; I knew He had put that truck driver and me together. As Scripture says, "The steps of a good man are ordered by the Lord" (Psalm 37:23, KJV). I, however, didn't know this would be just the beginning of what God would do in the days and years ahead.

Just a few days later I learned about wood stain that was available from Christian Appalachian Project (CAP), an interdenominational non-profit ministry that has served the people of Eastern Kentucky for several decades. All I had to do was to drive the eighty-five miles from Williamsburg to CAP's headquarters in Lancaster, Kentucky, pick it up, and deliver it to people who could distribute it. Of course, I did. The wood stain was not as important as the relationship with CAP that began that day. CAP began sending large quantities of food and other items to Cedaridge as well as began making introductions that opened the door for other groups to send things for us to distribute. In 2015, CAP is still a strong partner.

Understandably, when the merchants near our storefront saw what was happening they had doubts about our plans. One merchant asked me if we continued to bring in semi-loads of food and goods to be given away free, would that not mean that his business would suffer? God gave me a response: I asked him how many times he had seen 900 people in his store. If some of the people who came to our place for help spent even a little of the money in his store that they would normally have spent on the food we were giving away, would that not be more than they had previously spent there? He liked that answer.

Among the many things we received were semi-loads of 100-pound sacks of white potatoes, instant oatmeal, and grits. I vividly remember the joy of seeing needy people line up to receive much-needed food and of driving the ministry's pickup truck up and down the back roads and the hollers around Williamsburg to deliver food and household items to people without transportation to come to Cedaridge's building.

As volunteers and I made our way around the area for our deliveries, many living conditions broke our hearts. Many times we found six or more people ranging in age from babies to the elderly living in old beat-up school buses or run-down trailers surrounded by weeds, trash, and automobile tires. Many times we found they had no working cook stove, no indoor plumbing, and the only source of heat was a dangerous potbelly wood stove. As we talked with them, we tried hard to maintain their dignity. I would make casual conversation, affirming such things as fix-up projects the people were trying to do. I would talk with the children about things that interested them. Then, when we'd given them the food we'd brought, I would casually explain how to prepare it without having a working cook stove. I always told them it had been an honor to be with them and if Cedaridge could help with anything else, we'd love to do that. And I meant it. (In 2015, we still see similar living conditions and we still respond in the same way.)

When I needed to take pictures or videos of the ministries in which Cedaridge was involved to show potential donors, I always asked permission of the people involved. Most of the time, they would hesitate and say they didn't like to be in pictures, but then they would come around.

IN LATE 1993, after about a year in the Third Street storefront, we moved to what was known as the R.C. Bottling Plant on Second Street. For the first time, we had loading docks and a warehouse in which to store non-perishables. And we now had our own fork lift. What a God-send!

Prior to that time, we'd borrowed pallet jacks and forklifts from area businesses when we could, but more often than not our few volunteers and I would spend hours on end unloading semis. Sometimes we would work all night in order to make use of the borrowed jacks and lifts and in order to get ready to distribute the items the next day. I knew that had to change. I was concerned about how hard we all were working and about how many hours we were spending unloading trucks – hours we could have spent in other aspects of the ministry. But how could we afford a forklift? We simply had no money to buy one. I didn't know what to do.

Then one day a semi-load of white potatoes came in. After the volunteers and I had spent several long hours unloading the truck with a borrowed pallet jack, I looked intently at the volunteers. For all those hours, they'd been unloading potatoes from the truck onto the pallet jack, pushing the loaded pallet jack to a spot in the warehouse, unloading the potatoes – and then repeating the process over and over. As I looked at them, I saw just how sweaty and tired they really were. I thought, *"If we'd had a forklift, the task would have taken two to three hours."* Plus, I thought about the tasks we'd neglected that had needed to be done that day. I knew it was time to ask God to provide a forklift. I knew we didn't have the money, but I knew He did.

That night I looked through a catalogue with previously owned forklifts and found one for $1,600 in Lexington, about a hundred miles away. As I talked with the Lord about the situation, He told me, *"Go ask money from the people who have said you need a forklift."* I was so excited that in spite of the late hour I called a friend who had a transport business and asked him if he would pick up the one I'd chosen. As the Lord would have it, the friend, whose schedule was always full, had a cancellation in Lexington. He said he would be happy to pick up the forklift.

I must confess that in my excitement I lost track of the time and almost began calling everybody that night. (In those years, I was very naive.) When I finally did go to bed, I was still trying to think of everybody I could ask for money.

Then the Lord said, *"Go to sleep."*

And I did.

The next morning I got up like I was being shot out of a cannon. I was eager to get the day going and see what God was up to on our behalf. When I told my secretary my plan, she told me I needed to ask everybody I knew for money for the forklift, not just the people who had said we needed a forklift. I couldn't agree, because the night before the Lord had given me specific instructions to ask only those people who had told me we needed a forklift. I knew He was going to provide the money.

First, I called to see if the forklift was still available. It was. Acting on God's word to me, I bought it. Next, I set out to raise the $1,600 in one day. I thought if sixteen people would give $100 each, we would be okay.

As the end of the workday drew near, I had $800 in hand and $800 promised. Some people had given $50; some $100; some even more. The bottom line, however, was that I didn't have the full $1,600 in hand. So around 5 p.m., I went to a local bank and talked with the president about the situation. I asked if I brought him the $800 I had raised, would he allow me to write a check for $1,600 for the forklift and hold the check until I could bring him the other $800. The banker agreed and even donated $200 toward the purchase of the forklift. I knew God was at work on our behalf.

I left the bank happy – that is until I realized neither I personally nor Cedaridge had a checking account at that bank. Immediately, I went back to the bank to set things right only to discover the president had left for the day. When I told his secretary the situation – and told her I would open an account – she called the banker at his home. He told her to take the money I had in hand and then write a cashier's check for the full amount. He said that I could bring him the remainder of the money the next day.

By the next day, I had the money in hand from all the people who had promised to give. God had told me to ask money only of those who had said we needed a forklift, and I had obeyed. I believe that before I had even begun asking them to give, God had already put it on their hearts to help us get a forklift. Everyone I asked said, "Yes." With the additional $800 in hand, I happily went to the bank.

AFTER WE MOVED to the R.C. Bottling Plant, it didn't take long for Cedaridge to become a distribution point to area ministries and churches. We regularly began receiving semi-truck loads of food, furniture, and other goods, which we gladly passed on. God was confirming our mission.

One time, we received twenty tons of loose white potatoes. Several local volunteers and I shoveled and shoveled and distributed all of them. At about four pounds to a shovel, that's 10,000 shovels-full.

Another time, we received a semi-load of bottled water in gallons, pints, and quarts. My first impression was to distribute it immediately, but God had another plan. While I was thinking about and praying through how to distribute the water, I received a call from the Whitley County judge asking me if I had any bottled water on hand. When I told him I had a semi-load, he was thrilled. He told me that someone had intentionally contaminated the water supply for a community of eight of so families by pouring diesel fuel down the community's well. The judge said it would be at least a week before the well would be ready to use again, leaving the families without water in the meantime. He was more than happy to send the county Emergency Management Team (EMT) to pick up the water and distribute it to the families. A few days later, I called the judge to ask if more water was needed, and we gave another semi-load.

Often during those years because we had a large, dry warehouse we were able to store semi-loads of goods and wait to see where God would use them. I especially remember the winter of 1995. For three or four months, the snow came, then the ice came on top of the snow, and then more snow and ice, making travel treacherous and almost impossible. One day we received a semi-load of fresh white potatoes and canned food. We offloaded it into our warehouse, and I prayed about what to do with it. I knew many people in the county were iced in and couldn't get to the grocery store. I then felt led to call the county EMT to see if they could distribute the potatoes and canned goods. They did.

While many semi-loads were brought directly to our facility, often we were offered goods and food if we could pick up the items. On those occasions I would rent a 24-foot U-Haul truck and drive to the pick-up site. It was well worth the miles driven if it meant we would have more food and goods to distribute.

We continued to receive materials from Christian Appalachian Project. CAP provided all our office furniture. They provided paint, stain, and paper products, which we distributed to area ministries and churches. They sent pallets of Vacation Bible School and Sunday School literature, which we also gave to area churches.

CAP connected us with Feed the Children, which began providing canned food and fresh food, such as crates of green beans and sweet potatoes. All Cedaridge had to do was pay the shipping charges from their warehouse in Nashville. Sometimes Feed the Children even paid for shipping but when they didn't, we asked local churches to raise the money to pay the costs. When I knew a shipment was coming in, I would call a local church and those good folk would sponsor a load by paying the shipping costs.

During our years at the R.C Bottling Plant, the Society of St. Andrews in Virginia became a long-standing partner. Every spring since then the society has sent a semi-load of seed potatoes, which is about 900 fifty-pound bags. In the early years, I relied on word-of-mouth to get the news about the free seed potatoes out to the needy in the community. Later, I used our radio program (more about that in chapter five). Now in 2015,

I place a notice on my Facebook page. It's a great sight to behold when people show up at our building for those potatoes.

Through the Society of St Andrews, we connected with In Jesus' Name Ministry. Often, that group sent semi-loads of white potatoes.

Flexcon, headquartered in Michigan, regularly sent semi-loads of rolls of plastic to use to seal windows against the cold temperatures in winter and to seal the crawl space under homes.

Tile Cera, headquartered in Tennessee, sent a semi-load of ceramic tile almost every week. I appreciated their accountability system. In order for a family or a church to receive tile, they had to furnish a picture of the area to be tiled and then finish the project in thirty days. At the end of the thirty days, they had to send Tile Cera another picture showing that the tile had been used as proposed. If they hadn't finished the project, they were red-tagged, which meant they couldn't get any more supplies from Tile Cera until the project was completed and the red tag was removed. It was a great system which insured the tile was used as specified and not sold. CAP provided tile grout, and Feed the Children provided mortar and Wonderboard (tile backer board). These donations became especially important when the Lord opened an unexpected door to work on the area's sub-standard housing, which I will write about in chapter six.

Each Christmas for about ten years we received a semi-load of Kellogg's cereal, thanks to a local Catholic nun named Sister Leane Harris. When her health deteriorated, our connection to Kellogg's ended.

While our primary mission was to provide food and goods for area ministries and churches to distribute, we also continued direct-ministry as well. I remember one Thanksgiving when we provided 200 dinners, including turkeys, to needy families. At the time Cedaridge only had a few dollars in the bank, which wasn't nearly enough for such a project, but God provided. With each dinner, we included a gospel tract and we shared a word about the Lord.

I'm often asked how we screen the recipients of the things we give away. The answer is that because we distribute mainly to ministry groups and churches, we don't need to screen. All the ministries and churches with which we work are reputable, and because they actually hand out the items, they do the screening. We use the terms "Distributing" to describe what we do and "Sharing" to describe what the ministries and churches do.

DURING THOSE YEARS in the R.C. Bottling Plant building, our teenage son, Terry, was heavily involved in the ministry at Cedaridge. I remember one time when a woman called to ask if we had a couch she could buy. She came to the thrift store, paid a nominal amount for the hide-a-bed, and asked us to deliver it. That day the only people working at Cedaridge were Terry and me, so we loaded the couch onto our pickup and took it to her apartment. The entry to the apartment was so narrow that we had to turn that very heavy couch on end and work hard to squeeze it through the door. Plus, the woman had all kinds of what-nots everywhere in the apartment, so we were walking on eggshells the entire time, trying not to break anything. By the time we got the couch in and got it placed where she wanted it, it was late in the evening.

Lo and behold, the next morning she called. She ranted and raved about how we had sold her a couch that wasn't nearly worth the $20 she'd paid for it. She demanded that we come to her apartment that very minute and pick it up. We did, reversing the moving-in operation and once again trying to avoid all the what-nots.

About three hours later she called and asked us to bring the couch back to her. When I told Terry, he said, "No way," but for some reason I felt we should. So back we went.

After that, I didn't hear anything from her for a long time. Then one morning when I came into my office, my secretary told me that a woman had come in and asked to see me. When she'd learned I wasn't in, she'd said she'd be back later that day. When she came back, I didn't recognize her, as she looked totally different. She told me she had got saved and that the Lord had told her to come to see me and ask for my forgiveness for how she had treated Terry and me over the couch.

I immediately knew why I had felt in my spirit that Terry and I should take that couch back to her: Terry needed to learn that sometimes things are not as they seem. It wasn't about the couch; it was about waiting on the Lord to work in that woman's heart and for her to make things right with Him and then to make things right with Terry and me, her brothers in Christ.

A YEAR INTO our time at the R.C. Bottling Plant the family events about which I wrote in chapter three took place. While we were dealing with the growth of the ministry, Joyce, Terry, and I also were rejoicing in the adoption of Renee Joy and the birth of Holly Angel. And we were grieving at the death of Dad Teague. The year 1994 was filled with many highs and many lows in the Decker household.

BY 1996, WE THOUGHT we were set. Cedaridge had been in the R.C. Bottling Plant for about three years. We had loading docks; we had a forklift; we were receiving as many as eighty-two semi-loads of food and goods each year; we had a dry storage warehouse; we were the distribution center for about 400 churches and ministries in seven counties.

And then we learned that the city of Williamsburg planned to take the site of the R.C. Bottling Plant as part of land needed to build a flood wall. For the fourth time in as many years, Cedaridge Ministries would have to move.

The only suitable building we could find was what was called "The Bailey Building," which was a landmark in the community located at Exit 11 on Interstate 75. We bought the 22,000-square foot building with a bank loan and moved in March 1996.

---

LOOKING IN: *Janus Jones*
*When I first met Keith, he was just a teen-aged boy trying to find his place in the world. (He lived with my sister Carol Alderman and her husband, Norman, for five months of his sophomore year in high school.) I've seen Keith's ministry from the beginning when he preached his first sermon to where he is today in 2015. When Keith made a profession of faith and fell in love with Jesus, he fell in love with everybody else, too. It is almost amazing to have seen him develop from a teen-aged boy to where he is today.*

*Keith has always been a dreamer. The most amazing thing is how over the years he has learned how to flesh out his dreams and bring them to reality.*

Janus Jones
Retired Director of Missions
Mt. Zion Baptist Association
Williamsburg, Kentucky

# Five

The move to the Bailey Building in 1996 brought many blessings, but it also brought many problems. Because of its location, the building did give Cedaridge greater visibility. Because the Bailey Country Store which was located in the building had been a fixture in the area for more than thirty years, all we had to say was "Bailey Building" and people knew where to come. In fact, the store was such a beloved fixture that I'd hesitated to buy the building – I didn't want to be the one to shut it down.

But Cedaridge had bought the building and we had moved in. It wasn't long, however, before we learned that it came with a price for the ministry, our family, and me personally – and often the three were intertwined. Yet, in spite of the hardships, the Lord continued to use Cedaridge and I give Him praise for that.

Unbeknownst to me, the building posed a major health risk. When we bought it, I was aware of water problems in the basement and I knew the roof was in terrible shape. What I didn't know, however, was how quickly the water and the leaky roof would lead to more serious issues.

Not long after we moved in I learned just how bad the situation was when I developed major breathing problems. Many, many days I had to sit on the floor in my office and lean against a chair in order to breathe. The result was that over the first years we were in the Bailey Building I had to spend one to two weeks each year in the hospital. Each time, the doctors thought something was wrong with my heart, but my health problems persisted.

There were times during those years when I wasn't sure I was going to live. One Wednesday night when I was home alone, my breathing was so shallow that I couldn't even go to church. As the evening wore on, my breathing got worse and worse, and I finally called 911. I literally thought that was my last day on earth. As I waited for the ambulance, I looked up at a picture of Jesus that was hanging on our living room wall and prayed, *"Lord, if this is the end, then take care of my family."*

When the ambulance got to our street, the driver couldn't find our house, so the 911 operator called and asked me to turn on the porch light so the driver could locate it. Somehow, I managed to crawl to turn on the light. When the ambulance arrived, the technicians immediately began administering oxygen and rushed me to the hospital. My doctor urged me to go on 24-hour oxygen, but I didn't.

That time, I stayed in the hospital for a week. The next Wednesday, I was back home. Once again I was sitting on the couch, looking up at the picture of Jesus. Suddenly, the Lord told me He was sorry. I asked, *"Why? You don't make mistakes."* He replied, *"I'm sorry I couldn't take you."* At that moment I felt like the Apostle Paul when he said, "For to me to live is Christ, but to die is gain.… For I am in a strait betwixt the two, having a desire to depart, and to be with Christ; which is far better; Nevertheless to abide in the flesh is more needful for you" (Philippians 1:21, 23-24, KJV).

After the move to the Bailey Building, my epileptic seizures returned as well. I had one or two episodes a year. When I had an episode, I would fall down unexpectedly or I would be talking with someone or would be preaching at Corn Creek Church when suddenly my speech would slow and I would freeze. I told my people if that happened while I was in the pulpit, then they should guide me to a pew where I could lie down; I wouldn't be able to tell them what was happening or what to do. They were incredibly understanding. They embraced what I thought of as a major personal flaw and hindrance to being a pastor and saw it as an opportunity to minister to me even as I ministered to them. Instead of treating me as a leper to avoid, they did the opposite: Each time I had a seizure, they would gather around me. They didn't retreat.

If I had an episode in the middle of a worship service, the good people at Corn Creek would continue on with the service as if nothing had happened. I remember one Christmas play in particular. As I was greeting people and shaking hands before the service, I fell. The people went on with the play as scheduled. When I woke up and asked what had happened, I learned that when I had fallen I'd left my tooth print on the seat in front of me and the back of my shoe heels had pulled the trim off a pew behind me. Someone had sat beside me until I woke up. As usual, as soon as I woke up I was back to myself; we continued with the other planned activities.

Once again as when I had first been diagnosed, there were several periods of time when I couldn't drive. (By then, Kentucky law required only a three-month seizure-free period before an epileptic could get his or her license back. That was much better than the one-year period when I'd first been diagnosed years before.)

Finally, about four years after we'd moved to the Bailey Building, a retired international missionary came to volunteer with Cedaridge. She immediately realized the building had a major problem with dampness and mold and bought several dehumidifiers. Within a week, I was breathing some better. I, however, still had to make another trip to the hospital.

Looking back, I think the stress of the hardships of day-to-day ministry in the Bailey Building and the physical problems I encountered led to the flare-up of the epilepsy. And I think I was physically sick most of the seventeen years Cedaridge was located in the Bailey Building.

AS FOR CEDARIDGE, for almost all of those seventeen years we were housed at Bailey's, it was hard to keep the ministry going. Joyce, our children, and I were the only day-in-and-day-out workers. A few local volunteers did help from time to time, but very few helped on a regular basis. Often we were criticized for being disorganized and for being junky, which was hard for some volunteers to understand. The only response I could give was, "We're doing the best we can."

During those years, I tried many things both to minister more effectively and to help with Cedaridge's financial needs. Some of the things worked and some didn't. My philosophy was – and is – if the Lord wants me to try something, I have to try it no matter the result. If something doesn't work, I abandon it.

Cedaridge's finances were always tight, which meant often there was no money for gas, heat, or the electric bill. (At the time, our utility bills came to about $800 a month.) To keep costs down in the winter, Joyce, our children, and I wore our coats all the time we were in the building, and if the outside temperature dropped below 32 degrees, Joyce and the girls just stayed home while Terry and I went to the building. Regularly, we sold aluminum cans and cardboard to help pay the bills. Sometimes we had to take out bank loans to cover the ministry's basic expenses. Plus, Joyce and I often paid utility bills out of our own pocket.

Many, many times we didn't know where the money to pay a bill was going to come from until the very last minute. And then the Lord would lay it on the heart of someone to help. One time a woman showed up with a check for $1,400 for utilities. What a blessing! Most often, however, the money wasn't laid in our laps; we had to work for it repeatedly. It felt as if we were receiving manna for one day at a time much like the Israelites on their journey out of Egypt (Genesis 16). But never did the ministry come close to shutting down; we still had our mandate from the Lord.

Later I learned that through those difficult years some people in the community were watching us, expecting the ministry to close any day. They were ready to buy the Bailey Building.

As for our family's personal finances, from the beginning of Cedaridge until today, there never has been adequate funding for Cedaridge to pay me a full-time salary. My salary as pastor of Corn Creek Baptist Church has supplemented what I've received from Cedaridge. The uncertainty of our personal finances coupled with the ever-present needs of the ministry has always been harder on Joyce than on me. In spite of everything, she has continued to learn to trust the Lord to provide. I am thankful for her.

Over the years, when people have asked me, "How do you live?" I simply have said, "God has always provided." And He has.

IN THE MIDST OF ALL the building and ministry difficulties, four years into our Bailey Building years our family faced yet another personal crisis. In March 2000, arsonists robbed and then torched our home. We lost everything we owned. The loss was doubly hard because Dad Teague had left the house to us in his will – it was the house in which I'd lived in my last year of high school – and our family had lived there for about five years.

The night of the fire, Joyce and I remembered and grieved. We thought about her mom and dad, my mom and dad, Dad Teague, and friends and family. We thought about all the things they had given us, which were now gone. We thought about my awards from high school that were also gone. We thought about our children, who had lost their home.

In the days that followed, the memories of Dad Teague as well as all the memories of the good times Joyce and I and our children had enjoyed in that house were almost overwhelming. The fire and its aftermath was one of the lowest points in all my years of ministry. Needless to say, the loss was devastating for our daughters, Renee Joy and Holly. (Our son, Terry, was already on his own.) To this day, fifteen years later, Holly says each time she tops the hill above our home, she wonders if our new house will still be standing or if someone will have torched it, too. She was five years old when our house burned; today she is twenty.

Yet, as the Lord had done so often before at low points in our lives, He watched over our family. The day of the fire when I topped the hill and saw the smoke, He clearly spoke to me and said, *"I'll take care of it."* I took that to mean He would take care of everything. Over the next year and a half, I held tightly to that promise.

Looking back, I know the Lord already was taking care of us when the arsonist struck. Most importantly, that day Joyce and the girls were not at home. They were safe.

I know, too, that the Lord had made sure we had home owner's insurance. Until a few days before the fire, we'd never had insurance because we didn't think we could afford it. For some time, however, Joyce had felt the Lord telling her we needed to take out a policy. Then she asked for insurance for her wedding anniversary gift, and we got a policy on March 06. Our home burned to the ground on March 16.

Additionally, I know the Lord had prepared me for the fire just months before it happened. In early December I'd been privileged to take a trip to Israel, thanks to the generosity of a volunteer at Cedaridge. While in Israel, I had only one nighttime dream that I remembered and wrote down in my journal. In the dream, a man was going about a city wearing a garment with those old fashioned Big-Ben-type clocks with the big ringers on each side sticking all over it. At first, the clocks annoyed him, especially since more were being added as he moved about. It also seemed he'd been a regular person until a spiritual anointing had come over him; the anointing had been given so that he could tell people how to be saved. The man also had a special gift – he could fly. He would start running and moving his arms and then he would lift off the ground. One day a man asked him to ride with him to see a sick person, but he said, "No, I'll just fly." As he followed the car down the road, policemen and firemen began spraying him with foam, which hampered his flying. Some people began crying out for the men to leave him alone while others said they didn't want him to convert their people. Then as a fireman sprayed him, the man asked,

"But what if I am for real?" One of the policemen then told the man to fly up another street, which would be safer. At that point, he knew what the clocks were all about: God was telling him, *"You haven't got much time."*

And now, about three months after the Israel trip, our house burned. Before the arsonists set fire to our home, they ransacked it and took many items. As the Lord would have it, they left my black suitcase with my journal and papers from Israel in a pile behind our house. A couple of days after the fire, as people were helping us sort through the remains, a friend found the bag and brought it to me. The bag had been unzipped, but nothing was missing. Immediately, I remembered my dream, which had occurred in Joppa where Peter had his famous dream (Acts 10). As I recalled my dream, I thought about how I'd always been told that when someone dreams about being able to fly, it means that he or she has a really good relationship with the Lord. I also thought about how I'd dreamed about being able to fly ever since I was a teen. I found great comfort in those thoughts.

Still, it seemed to Joyce and me that God had wiped out everything from our previous life. Except for that black suitcase, we had very little with which to start over. It was a sad, depressing thought. In the weeks that followed, however, I saw why God had preserved that black bag when He began opening the door for me to talk about my trip to Israel in local schools. My journal, a bottle of water I'd collected from the Jordan River, stones I'd picked up, and other mementos helped me tell my story. I knew then if the bag had burned, its contents couldn't have been replaced. I thought back to another part of my dream: A black energy pack had allowed the man to continue to fly when everything and everyone was trying to pull him down. I knew my black suitcase was my energy pack.

AFTER THE FIRE, for the first time in a long time Joyce and I weren't the givers. Instead, we were the receivers. Looking back, it's awesome how the people at Corn Creek Church as well as people in the community and beyond rallied around us. We were the needy and God took care of us through His people.

Within days a man with whom I had spent many days and nights when I was growing up came to see me and told me how the Lord had awakened him during the night to tell him to build us a house. Knowing how Gorman Frazier trusted the Lord daily for guidance was very special to me and my family during those hard days. When he took Joyce and me to see the type of houses God had laid on his heart for us, we were in awe. We both thought they all were much nicer than we could afford or could ever dream of having for our family. But Gorman insisted he'd heard a sure word from the Lord about what He wanted for us.

So we began to pray and work on the house plans. Joyce had always wanted a bigger kitchen and I had wanted a second bathroom. Through the years Joyce has asked for very little and she never once has said that God is not able to provide, so when I asked Gorman to enlarge the kitchen plans, he gladly did – and he added a second bathroom. Over the following weeks, Joyce, the girls, and I had a great time working out where each room was going to be. With Gorman's guidance, we came up with the design for our house.

With the insurance money we received, Joyce and I began the rebuilding process but were only able to raise the shell of the house. In the meantime, someone gave us a camper/trailer for our family of four. We were very thankful for it, because we had nothing, We lived in that crowded camper for two months until I bought a mobile home with money the insurance company had given us to live on until we could get back on our feet. We parked the mobile home on our property so we could be near our new house as it was being built. Granted, the mobile home was a fixer-upper, but at least it was larger than the camper. I planned to donate it to Cedaridge to give to someone in need after our house was rebuilt.

In the wake of the fire our family not only learned to receive and not just give but we also learned just how much a faith ministry such as Cedaridge needs a strong support network. In 1999, we had begun to work on building such a network when Larry Martin, Missions Team Leader for the Kentucky Baptist Convention headquartered in Louisville, had come to visit Cedaridge and had encouraged me to become a Southern Baptist Mission Service Corps (MSC) missionary. He'd explained that while a MSC missionary doesn't receive a salary and must provide his or her own financial support, the connection would open the door for Southern Baptists who lived out of the area to hear about Cedaridge and to inquire about how to become involved. I'd known Larry since about 1995 and had grown to love and appreciate him for his love for the Lord and his wisdom in how to serve the Lord, so I'd gladly agreed to become MSC and had attended orientation. I was learning the Lord was moving Cedaridge and me into another phase of ministry, one that would connect me with many other people who love the Lord.

At MSC orientation, Larry had asked each of us to tell about our ministries. When my turn came, I'd felt compelled by the Lord to talk about the future of Cedaridge instead of its past. I shared how I felt the Lord would transform Cedaridge through prayer. In the weeks after the orientation, I talked with Larry about enlisting prayer partners from near and far to pray for our ministry. I made lists and contacted people – and I waited for change to come at Cedaridge. Nothing happened. I didn't understand why until I began to see that the Lord wasn't just telling me to enlist prayer partners for the ministry. More importantly, He was enlisting me to pray more than I had ever prayed in my life. Looking back, I know He was preparing me for the trials and blessings that would bring me to my knees many times over the coming years, and He was preparing me for answers to my prayers that could only come from Him.

Less than a year after MSC orientation I experienced first-hand how important my own prayers, the prayers of other believers, and a support team are. A few months after the fire, Larry sent Bruce Byce and three men from South Carolina to see what was going on with us. They came, looked at our situation and said they found it very depressing. For one thing, we had no working water faucets or shower in our mobile home. The men went back to South Carolina and through a partnership between Saluda Baptist Association in Anderson, South Carolina, and Mission Development Ministries of which Bruce is president, raised about $12,000 to buy materials; then they brought volunteers to finish our house. We celebrated Christmas 2000 in our new home, even though it wasn't totally finished. What a blessing! Over the years since, Bruce and his wife, Kathy, have brought hundreds of mission volunteers from South Carolina as well as food, building materials, and all manner of supplies to Cedaridge. They've been some of our strongest supporters.

No doubt about it: The fire was devastating. No doubt about it: God saw us through and taught us many lessons. He was with us.

THERE'S NO OTHER way to say it but that the seventeen years at the Bailey Building were scary and difficult times for my family and me. Day after day I would go to my office, get down on my knees and claim the Scripture that says, "The effectual, fervent prayer of a righteous man availeth much" (James 5:16, KJV). I'd certainly learned the importance of praying. Never once, however, did I say that Cedaridge Ministries should fold; I just knew God had more in store. I knew no matter what my mind was telling me about the future of the ministry or no matter how my mind was telling me I wasn't of much use to God or anybody, my spirit – God's Spirit – was telling me that one way or another, God would make a way out.

Again, just as when I'd been a six-month old baby and when I'd been abandoned by my family at age seventeen, it was only by the grace of the Lord and the loving help of people whom He used that I survived. Since then, friends and volunteers have told me they, too, didn't think I would make it. But, once again, God heard my cry from the mountains.

One such friend is the secretary of Cedaridge's Board of Directors, Brenda Mack. She recalls a time when she came to my office in the Bailey Building to find me "lower than I've ever seen him." (That's saying a lot since she's known me since high school and has been involved with the ministry from day one.) When she asked what was wrong, she says I responded, "Sister Brenda, I don't know what to do. I don't know if I should stay and try to make it work or if the Lord is through with me."

Brenda laid hands on me and prayed over me that day. She asked the Lord to send someone to help if He wanted me to continue with the ministry. She asked the Lord to guide and direct me and help me know what I needed to do – and to let me know clearly.

Brenda asked other people to pray, too, and they did. Not long after, the local county court began sending people to work off their community service in our recycling center, which we had begun in 1994 by baling and selling left-over clothing from the thrift shop. We desperately needed those workers.

Then God used a mission team to help me hold on. About a month before a preview team from a church in Powder Springs, Georgia, came to plan a mission trip, everything seemed to cave in on me. Except for the community-service people in the recycling center, only Joyce and I were working in the ministry, and we simply couldn't keep up with all that needed to be done. Things continued to be a mess in and around the building, plus Cedaridge had fallen behind on paying bills. Each day, all I could ask the Lord was just to get me through that day. I prayed more than I'd ever prayed in my life. I prayed for myself, for my family, and for the ministry. It felt as if it was just me and the Lord carrying a very heavy load.

Things were very bad and yet as the famous anonymous poem "Footprints in the Sand" says, "The times when you've seen only one set of footprints is [sic] when I [the Lord] carried you." I knew that, but often I didn't feel it.

Between the time when the preview group came and the work group came, I prayed each day for the Lord to help me, and I literally counted off the days until they were scheduled to arrive. Every time I began to think negatively, the Lord always reminded me that He had told me I was never to give up.

And then the Powder Springs team arrived and got to work. They pressure washed the outside of our building; they cleaned the inside; they cleaned up the area around the building. Those Georgians lifted a burden off me.

Looking back, that was yet another period of maturing spiritually for me. Unlike the chastisement of epilepsy when I was younger, this time I believe God put me through a trial to test me to see if I was ready for a greater ministry He wanted to open. I believe God always puts His children through trials before He promotes them. He wants to see if we are ready for the new challenge. In years yet to come, I would learn the greater the trial, the greater the blessing.

Things began to look up. Somehow, I began to believe in myself again.

LET ME BE CLEAR: The Lord gave Joyce and me many enjoyable ministry experiences to boost our spirits during the years in the Bailey Building. I married several couples in the building. One time, I even married a couple in the aisle of our Country Store/thrift shop. It seems that the couple had gone to the County Court Clerk's office to get married but decided they wanted a minister to marry them instead. So the clerk called me and asked if I would marry them. Since the only available space at Cedaridge was the Country Store, they said "I Do" right there amid the racks of clothes.

Then there were volunteers like Imogene Frechette from Corn Creek Church who always lifted our spirits. She worked long and hard helping distribute food and goods to churches and ministries – a task she dearly loved. One day she had to leave early to attend some function – but not before I told her we would be receiving a truckload of items that night. She immediately told me she wouldn't be at home but to "just leave them on my carport." I said, "Okay," but I didn't tell her that it would be a 24-foot truckload. I left the load. Sure enough, she distributed every last item.

Plus, there were those experiences which can only be described as miracles. For example, for about ten years we'd been praying that Dove Broadcasting Company would get involved in the Cedaridge ministry. For several years at Christmas time, the company had sent three semi-loads filled with clothing, food, and toys into other parts of Appalachia. Each time they distributed items to as many as 3,000 people in venues such as school gyms or civic centers. For several years, one of their drivers had been praying that Cedaridge could host an event in Williamsburg. We thought we could handle 3,000 people.

You can imagine how thrilled we were when Dove decided to come to Williamsburg. The only hitch was that usually the company gave a one-year notice, but we'd have only three months to get ready. Immediately we set to work. I asked the mayor of Williamsburg to help pull together the various helping agencies and the public school resource centers personnel to make it happen.

When we began looking for a place large enough to hold the Give-A-Way, we soon realized the Williamsburg civic center could only hold 300 people and the local armory could only hold 600. So we asked the Whitley County school superintendent if we could use the high school gymnasium, and he agreed. He, however, forgot to tell the school principal, who had scheduled a basketball tournament in the gym for the weekend of our Give-A-Way.

As for me, I knew God was in Dove's coming, so the tournament didn't faze me. I knew He would make a way. We, however, did have to alter our plans a bit. Instead of setting up for the Sunday afternoon event during the day on Saturday, we had to set up after 9 p.m. on Saturday after the tournament was over – which meant more than half of our scheduled volunteers couldn't help because of the late hour and needing to get ready for church the next day. (I had to preach the next morning, too.)

After a very long night, somehow it all worked out. Then a big snow fell on Sunday morning, resulting in very bad road conditions. In our area, people just don't travel when the mountain roads are icy and snow-covered so we weren't sure how many would show up that afternoon. Were we ever surprised! Even if no snow had fallen we were expecting no more than 3,000. Instead, 7,000 people showed up. We filled the gym twice. All afternoon it seemed that at least as many people were waiting their turn outside in the snow as were inside at any given time.

At the end of the day as we wrapped up the event we realized that we'd just experienced a loaves-and-fishes miracle. The volunteers from Dove Broadcasting had brought enough gifts for 3,000 people, but they had served 7,000! Plus, they had two box-truck loads of clothing and toys left over. Of course, we distributed those leftovers to people who hadn't been able to come.

Another enjoyable experience (several years of enjoyable experiences to be truthful) came with a long-running thirty-minute five-day-a-week radio program we inherited when we bought the Bailey Building. For many years Bart Bailey had been the king of the show. After we bought the building, Janus Jones and I shared that title. To this day, when I mention the program people ask me to repeat the program's opening spiel, which was done auctioneer-style. Here's how it went, as I remember it:

*Good morning, Southeast Kentucky. This is Bailey's Request Show coming to you live from Cedaridge Ministries located here on the beautiful banks of Briar Creek where all the crawdads wear tuxedos and they have the big Yacht and Country Club. Set back in your easy chair, take you another good ole sip of that coffee, grab you another hot biscuit, maybe a piece of tenderloin, good old red sop. Put some jam or jelly in the middle of it. Enjoy yourself.*

*We gonna be here for the next thirty minutes to talk about items to buy, sell, or trade; tell you about some things going on in the community; give you where the signs are; play you a song; and maybe a few other things. Tell you about a few church announcements and other things going on in Southeast Kentucky. Always remember life's too short to take it too fast, so slow down a little bit and enjoy yourself.*

A note: Red sop is what we mountain folk call red-eye gravy – the gravy made with strong coffee and the grease from frying country ham. The signs of the moon are used to indicate the best days to plant crops, among other things.

For thirty minutes, we'd take calls, talk, and have a great time. We usually had a trivia question for the listeners. I remember one that caused our phone lines to go wild. That day, as usual, I'd gotten the trivia from the *Farmers' Almanac*. It went like this: What is the fastest insect? The answer is the mosquito, which can travel 75 miles per hour except during mating season when the housefly wins the contest at 95 miles per hour.

No problem, right? Well, listener after listener called to say they couldn't believe a preacher would say such a thing on the air. I have to admit I was devastated, so I decided to go to the expert radio host, Bart Bailey, to learn if any of his listeners hadn't liked anything he'd said. He laughed and said, "Yes. Just get tough skin and move on." I took his advice.

The show always ended with *"Clock's got. We gotta git. Have yourself a good day. We'll be back here again tomorrow. Bye-bye."*

Janus and I kept the show going for about ten years. After that, I ran it for about a year. Now, it's just a fond memory.

During the Bailey Building years, my hands-on ministry brought me much satisfaction. (In 2015, it still does.) When food came in, I would find anyone who could go with me to distribute it. We'd start out up a holler with a load and return with nothing. One time, I remember hand-shoveling two semi-loads of potatoes into bags and then delivering them to drop sites in local communities.

Often after Cedaridge had hosted Christmas Give-A-Way events, we had what we called Finding Christmas. I would load the leftovers in my pick-up truck and begin praying about who the Lord knew needed Christmas. He would say to me, *"Drive slow. Turn up this holler. Stop at this house."* Always, the people were the very ones who needed the things I had. After a few years, I had to use a box truck instead of my pick-up truck in order to hold all the leftovers. Reporting on Finding Christmas, a local newspaperman wrote, "Yes, there really is a Santa Claus." For me, to know we'd delivered items to people whom the Lord had told us to visit brought great comfort that He could still use me as His servant. Yes, the Lord was still in control.

I also found great joy in helping families with small fix-up jobs. I began a practice that I've continued to this day. I always carry three tool boxes with me: one with electrical tools, one with plumbing tools, and one with carpentry and basic tools. When I'm out in the communities or up the hollers checking out needs, I always try to determine if there are things I can fix on the spot. Many times, especially if someone else is with me, I make minor repairs. (Funny thing, when the winter weather turns bad, I never have any problem going up snow-or-ice-covered hills or maneuvering through deep mud. People often say the Lord is with me because I can go places most people can't. Between the Lord and those tool boxes, my vehicle has great traction.) Because I never know what repair situations I might get involved in, I always carry a change of clothes with me. I've often needed to change before a meeting or before going to lead services at Corn Creek Church.

Often I've been overwhelmed when I ask about someone's number one need. For example, one woman's house had been severely damaged in a storm, but all she asked was for me to replace a weak board in front of her kitchen sink. The weak spot was so small I could hardly find it. I'd thought she would ask for the siding on the house to be repaired and the inside rooms to be painted. Another homeowner asked for caulking around her windows; I'd thought the house needed underpinning and a new roof. Still another woman's water lines had broken and all she wanted was water reconnected to her commode. She didn't even mention getting water to the kitchen or replacing missing flooring or adding underpinning and insulation or putting on sheetrock, any of which I'd thought would be number one.

As I said, in 2015 I still carry those tool kits. I still find joy in personally making small repairs.

IN SPITE OF all the obstacles – including many, many more that I haven't recounted in these pages – the ministry grew during the early Bailey Building years. We expanded beyond Whitley County to include nine counties. The number of churches and ministry groups we passed food and goods on to grew to around 400. Without any publicity other than word-of-mouth, we continued to receive about ninety semi-loads of food and goods each year. By 1998, we were receiving approximately 5,000 pounds of clothing and serving more than 500 people through our Country Store/thrift shop each year. Selling the thrift shop items at nominal cost not only provided dignity for the people who used the shop but the money also helped with the ministry's utility bills. (Items in the thrift store have always been free for people in severe need.)

An added blessing was our relationship with the Bailey family, who were always supportive of all Cedaridge was doing. They helped us with fundraising and let us use their barn for our recycling enterprise. Bart and Ada Lee Bailey were great friends. Bart gave me the great gift of being a listening ear as the ministry grew.

Then the downturn in the U.S. economy around 1998 changed the ministry. Quickly, the yearly number of semi-loads of food and goods we received dropped to nineteen. Companies simply didn't have as much to give away. The downturn hit local churches as well, which meant they no longer had money to help us with freight charges. Also, we didn't have a loading dock at the Bailey Building, which affected the number of loads we could receive.

WAS CEDARIDGE'S ministry in jeopardy? What would the future of Cedaridge be?

Looking back, I now see how God had already begun opening another door of ministry for Cedaridge. Frankly, I hadn't expected to get involved in addressing the substandard housing needs in our area, but once again the Lord had different plans.

---

LOOKING IN: *Joyce Decker*
*Two of the hardest things I've had to deal with in all the years Keith and I have been married have been his epilepsy and the ever-present uncertainty of our personal finances. Still, in everything that has happened over the years we have ministered together, this Scripture in Lamentations has brought me great comfort. I have it posted on my refrigerator door so that I can read it each day.*

*It has become my life verse: "It is of the Lord's mercies that we are not consumed, because his compassions fail not. They are new every morning: great is thy faithfulness. The Lord is my portion, saith my soul; therefore will I hope in him"* (Lamentations *3:22-24, KJV*).

Joyce Decker
Cedaridge Ministries

# Six

Cedaridge's first housing project came unexpectedly in 1994 when a group from Kansas City, Missouri, contacted Mountain Outreach, a ministry of Cumberland College, about coming to the area to work on a house. Because Mountain Outreach had already filled its quota of projects for that year, the group's leaders referred the Missouri team to Cedaridge. The group came and painted the outside of the home of a neighbor of one of Cedaridge's board members.

After that, the Lord seemed to move us more and more into housing. After I became a Mission Service Corps missionary in 1999, the number of inquiries both from in-state and out-of-state church groups wanting to come on short-term summer mission trips grew rapidly. Initially five or so groups came each summer, but soon as many as twenty groups were coming. When many expressed interest in working directly with needy people, addressing the substandard housing needs was the answer.

Groups would work on houses during the daytime and then conduct Vacation Bible Schools or Backyard Bible Clubs each night. Often, they would lead evening worship services. They provided almost all the funding for their projects, with occasional funding help from Kentucky Housing and the Kentucky Baptist Convention. One summer early on in our housing efforts, volunteers working through Cedaridge built one house from the ground up and repaired twenty-two others.

The substandard housing we saw broke our hearts, and the ways in which God worked to use His people to address housing needs affirmed the direction the ministry of Cedaridge was going. This is best told through the stories of some of the people we've helped. Three of the most poignant stories date from the early days of our involvement in housing.

### Miss Mandy

WHEN I TOOK a mission preview team to visit Manda Senters to find out what she needed and how we could help, I asked her to name her five most pressing needs – something I always try to do, by the way. She quickly said that her number one need was "Tape."

You see, Mrs. Senters – Mandy, as she is called – was living in a one-room house that she herself had built from lumber from an abandoned building she had torn down. She'd covered the outside of her house with tarpaper and had put on rolled roofing. She told us she'd planned to build a two-room house, but thieves had stolen the extra lumber from her yard before she could get the second room up.

As we sat with her that autumn day, we could see she was doing the very best she could in a not-so-good situation. All her earthly possessions – a couch, a heating/cooking stove, a bed, and a few clothes and dishes – were clean and neat. She obviously took great pride in what she had.

Mrs. Senters explained that she wanted to tape the seams in the cardboard that formed the inside walls and ceiling of the house because wasps lived in the cracks and dropped down on her bed and her other belongings. Plus, she said taping the seams would help save on heating costs in the upcoming winter.

The mission team members were stunned, to say the least, and told her they would help. Mrs. Senters was so grateful that she offered to fix them a meal of chicken and dumplings and blackberry cobbler with berries she'd picked herself. We told her we'd take her up on her offer when we had finished the project.

Later that day, as the team and I debriefed and made plans to help Mrs. Senters, many were in tears. "We've got so much, and this lady is only concerned with getting tape," one team member said. None of them could believe she wanted to fix them a meal since she lived on about $60 a month.

We took her the tape and the group promised they would go back to their church – Shadowbrook Baptist in Suwanee, Georgia – raise the necessary funds, and return the following spring to fix her house.

Not long after that, I learned that when the group shared Mrs. Senters' story with their church, a revival broke out. They raised $5,000 through one spaghetti dinner alone! Eventually, they raised $10,000. They made plans to put vinyl siding on the outside of Mrs. Senters' house, add a bedroom, and spruce up the inside of the existing room. But there was one problem: Mrs. Senters' coal pile was on the exact spot where the bedroom needed to go. When I talked with Mrs. Senters about that, she said it was okay to move the coal, but before I could move it, she had it moved.

By the following summer of 1996, the church had raised the needed money. Then someone from the church called me with another idea: If Mrs. Senters could get enough land, the mission team would build her a brand new house instead of trying to fix up and add on to her one room. Her daughter and son-in-law, Trula and Charles Matlock, who lived in a simple house next door, happily agreed to give her a portion of their land.

Before the Shadowbrook team arrived to build the house, several members of Corn Creek Church and I marked off the site and poured the footer for the foundation. Then a group of adults from Shadowbrook Church came and poured the foundation, complete with a Bible in the cornerstone. Two weeks later, thirty-one youth and their adult chaperones came, and in one week they built Mrs. Senters a new house with a combination living room-kitchen, two bedrooms, and a bathroom. Shadowbrook Church also bought new kitchen appliances, kitchen and bathroom cabinets, linoleum, and carpet, which Mrs. Senters' daughter Trula installed. The church bought new furnishings as well. Women at Shadowbrook who weren't able to come to Kentucky even made curtains for the house. Mrs. Senters' old one-room house could now be used for storage.

On July 25, 1996, the electricity was turned on. No longer would Mrs. Senters' need to run an extension cord to her daughter's house next door to access electricity. Trula says that throughout the entire building process her mom "was really like a child getting a new toy. Each day she got more excited."

When the house was completed, Mrs. Senters kept her promise to cook a meal for the volunteers, most of whom were teenagers. I told them to graciously accept whatever she offered and explained they might think they were doing her a favor by asking her not to spend her precious money on them, but that would not be so. In true Appalachian fashion, if they refused her gift of a meal, Mrs. Senters wouldn't be able to receive their gift of a new house with the right spirit. If they refused her meal, she would think she wasn't good enough for them and that they were looking down on her. I told them they should gladly accept what she would set before them as a way of preserving Mrs. Senters' dignity. Believe me, they enjoyed every bite of that meal and she enjoyed cooking it for them.

"Mom was beside herself with happiness," Trula says. "And after the house was finished, she was simply delighted."

For many on that youth team, finishing Mrs. Senters' house was an experience they would never forget. In fact, one of the girls returned every summer through her college years to work with Cedaridge, and she always visited Mrs. Senters. One adult team member, Cathy Edwards, has stayed in touch with Mrs. Senters and her daughter through the years. (Cathy's reflections on her experiences are included at the end of this chapter.) Trula says that getting to know the volunteers who worked on her house was the highlight of her mother's life.

Sadly, in 2015 at 82 years of age, Mrs. Senters is very feeble. Among other things, she has cancer and Alzheimer's. But Trula says her mom has a strong desire to live, so she keeps plugging on. Recently Trula called me to say that Mrs. Senters wants me to conduct her funeral when she dies.

As I look back on Mrs. Senters' story, I realize that God was still teaching me to look at people through their own eyes before I saw them through my eyes – just as He had when my brother David and I had talked for the first time about my growing-up years. If I had gone to Mrs. Senters' house and assessed her needs myself, I would never have thought her number one need was tape. Looking back, the experience with her reinforced what God had begun to put on my heart: If I do the number one thing, then I am assured that everything else He does will just be icing on the cake.

### Granny on the Hill

ONE DAY MY son, Terry, and I were distributing food and looking in on people in the Faber community outside Corbin when I decided to check out one of the houses where I'd lived as a child. I didn't even know if the little red house on the hill – as we had called it – still stood, but as we neared the site I saw smoke curling out of the chimney and chickens scratching around in the front yard. It still stood and someone lived there.

That day Terry and I met Cora, who later came to be called Granny on the Hill. In her late 80s, she had lived in that red faux brick-sided house for many years. By that time, she left her house on the hill only once a year to have her eyes checked. Her children brought groceries and saw to her other needs. Often they'd offered to help her find a better house, but because she paid only $10 a month rent, she didn't want to move. As I got to know her, she said she always told her family she "had the Lord and He's looking over me." She would pause a long time and then say, "If they find a house that's cheaper, I might move." Another long pause. "But I don't think I'd take one for $5 a month." The little red house on the hill was home.

To be sure, the house had seen better days, so Terry and I offered to enlist mission groups to help her make it more livable. She agreed. One mission group painted the tarpaper that covered the inside walls. They cleaned everything. They built a ramp out the back door, which for the first time in many years enabled Cora to go to the outhouse without having to go out the front door and walk around the house.

The house was still nothing fancy, but Cora was very happy with it. "I've got a new house," she told me. "I never dreamed I'd have something this nice." The look on her face was priceless. Over the years Cora almost became a part of my family. When I visited her or when I took mission teams to see her, she always was happy to show off her house. She loved to laugh and she loved to talk about her growing-up days. It was a member of one of those teams who first called her "Granny on the Hill" and the name stuck.

Cora often said one of the hardest things she'd dealt with was that she had outlived many of those whom she loved, including her husband, several children, and several grandchildren. After saying that, she'd always pause. Then she'd say, "Things change." Another pause. Then, "But we can expect change."

For Cora, the one thing that didn't change was her faith in God. A strong Christian, she read her Bible every night. Until her death at age 94, she knew God was still watching over her.

### Arnold and Martha

SOMETIME AROUND the fall of 1998, a local politician named Everett Rains along with Bart Bailey were campaigning up a holler when they came upon a situation that blew their minds. They saw a log cabin they simply couldn't believe anybody could be living in, but they found that two people were. Soon after that, Bart called me to ask what I knew about the situation and to ask what could be done. He also said he and Everett wanted to wait until after the election was over to get involved; they didn't want to turn the situation into political theatre.

After the election was over, I went with the two men to visit Arnold and Martha for the first time. What we found was sheer squalor. The first things we saw as we walked up to their two-room frontier log cabin were piles and piles of coal and wood in the yard. We later learned that Arnold walked the roads, picking up coal and wood that had fallen from coal and logging trucks to use as fuel to heat their house. We also learned the cabin was one of the first log houses ever built in the area.

As for the cabin, for a window there was only a hole over which slats had been haphazardly nailed on the outside of the house. As for making contact with Martha and Arnold, the protocol was to go to the window-hole and call for them. Then they would come to the door, unlock a chain, come outside, re-chain the door on the outside, and sit on the rock steps to talk. Then, if they chose to, they would let you go inside. Over the years, local kids had made a habit of throwing rocks at the cabin and harassing them, so they didn't trust anybody. In fact, they kept their few valuables in the trunk of Arnold's old car.

When Arnold and Martha finally asked the three of us in, what a sight we encountered! Just getting through the two rooms was like walking a trail. Birds had built nests in the house. Everything in the kitchen was covered with dirt – Arnold explained that none of the things in the kitchen had been used since his father's death more than twenty years earlier. A shotgun and shells stood ready by the door in case anyone tried to get inside. The fireplace, which was the only source of heat or way to cook, was so small that a lump of coal just barely fit inside.

As we talked, we learned there was no safe water source on the place – someone had intentionally contaminated the well by throwing scrap metal and rotting meat in it. Arnold had to drive sixteen miles to Jellico, Tennessee, to get water from a spring.

As for refrigeration, the lower section of their ancient 1950s-era refrigerator hadn't worked in years. The freezer section, however, did work, so they put their medications and food as close as possible beneath the freezer section and stacked newspapers under the items to try to keep them cold.

Martha's bed was under the window-hole covered with the haphazard slats. Actually, the bed was a piece of foam placed on top of a sheet of plywood. Underneath the plywood were bottles, coal, old furniture – you name it. A quilt covered it all, which made the bed level with the window-hole.

When I asked Martha and Arnold what their number one need was, Arnold said he would like for Martha to have "a proper bed". Everett, Bart, and I told him we could see to that. When we talked with him about building them a better house, Arnold reluctantly agreed but set some terms for the deal. First, he said we couldn't tear the cabin down. You see, it had been his home from the time he was five years old, and he was now in his late fifties. The house plus five or so acres had been given to Arnold's dad to settle a $300 debt around 1945. Before his family had moved into the cabin, they had lived on the Whitley County poor farm, a place for indigent families to live and work. Second, Arnold said we couldn't move the coal and wood piles. I think being able to set those restrictions helped him maintain a degree of dignity. We agreed to the deal.

We also learned that Arnold and Martha weren't related. Arnold had taken Martha in a few years before when she'd become afraid for her safety at the place where she was living. She was now in her forties.

That winter, I did the leg work in preparation for building the house. Then, when spring came, over a six-week period six volunteer mission groups, including Youth on Mission and Baptist groups across the south, joined members of Corn Creek Church and myself in cleaning the area around the cabin. We separated the coal and wood into piles and built four lean-to shelters to store the fuel. We hauled away mounds of garbage that had been accumulating down the hill behind Arnold and Martha's house. Because they had no garbage pick-up, they'd just tossed their trash over the hill. We replaced their dilapidated outhouse with a new one. We tore down an out-building. We tried to clean the inside of the house. That brought some scary moments when we found a poisonous mother copperhead snake and her babies in the kitchen. And, yes, we got Martha a proper bed.

That spring, I dug the footer for the foundation. Then Clinton Petrey and other volunteers from Corn Creek Church laid the block foundation for the new house. After the groups had cleaned the area, other groups came in to build the house. I remember one youth group in particular. Now, they weren't the most experienced group; in fact, most of the group had never hit a nail. But as the Lord would have it, an engineer came with them. He laid out every piece of lumber for the house and closely supervised the youth as they cut each piece before they nailed the pieces together – a perfect fit every time. We used house plans from Mountain Outreach. (We've continued to use their house plans for all our construction projects since.)

In the early stages of working on the house, neighbors would come by to ask who had died. You see, they'd never seen so many people visit Arnold and Martha before and naturally thought all the activity meant a death in the family. Sadly, some locals continued to throw rocks at the house. Finally I'd had enough, so I took a can of green spray paint and wrote the words "Jesus Cares" on the side of the house. After that, there were no more questions or rocks.

And then as we were nearing completion of the two bedrooms, bath, living room, and kitchen, it all became too much for Arnold. Too many people around, too much activity, too much attention, I guess. He began to get defensive. And so when the house was about 98 percent complete with little left to do except install kitchen cabinets and doors, hook up the water, and complete a septic system, we had to stop.

I continued to visit Arnold and Martha, but for many years I didn't know that Arnold had boarded up the back half of the house, which included his bedroom, Martha's bedroom, and the bathroom. You see, each time I visited we sat in the front room and I just assumed they were using the entire house. After I did learn about the situation, I tried to assure Arnold that while the house was his to do with as he wished, I hoped he and Martha would live in all of it. His response was always something like this, "I ain't never had nothing that nice and I'm afraid of getting it dirty. I ain't worthy of such a house." He also would say that the electricity to heat the house would cost too much. (When we'd turned on the electricity for the first time, Arnold hadn't known how to turn on a light switch.)

For years, Arnold and Martha continued to sleep and eat in the old log cabin. Once in a while, they would sit in the new house in the daytime. They continued to use the outhouse.

For most who read this story, not being willing to move into a brand new house will be hard to understand, but once again as with other stories in this book, you need to know a bit about the Appalachian culture. The reasons were much deeper than the surface story Arnold told. Like most Appalachians, he was a proud mountaineer. In earlier years, he had worked for a living. He'd been a sharecropper on a farm, worked in a coal mine, worked as a janitor in a hospital, and been employed at several other jobs. He'd been self-sufficient and independent. In spite of his current living conditions, he didn't want charity.

For years, I continued to visit Arnold and Martha and offer whatever help Cedaridge could provide. Then one day, about ten years after work had stopped on the house, a new girl came to town. Angie Howard was the site director for the University of the Cumberlands (formerly Cumberland College) chapter of the national Southern Baptist Convention's youth on mission program called M-Fuge. When I first took Angie to meet Arnold and Martha, I was surprised at how quickly they welcomed her. Actually, they thought she was my daughter, and we never told them anything different. It was evident from the first that Angie cared deeply about people and about Arnold and Martha in particular. Another Appalachian culture tip: If Appalachians know you really care and are willing to spend time with them, they will, in turn, be willing to let you into their lives. Angie would sit and talk for as long as Arnold and Martha wanted. Before long, they agreed to let her line up groups to finish the house, and before long they moved in. For the five years Angie was M-Fuge site director, she continued to visit them and bring volunteers to help them. She often said that so many M-Fugers came to see Arnold and Martha that the two had become poster children for M-Fuge.

The most important part of this story happened in 2012: Martha and Arnold got saved. Arnold told me, "I've heard enough about that place down there [hell] that I don't need to go down there to check it out." I baptized Martha at Corn Creek Church, but Arnold would never agree to be baptized. He died in 2014. (In 2015, Martha is in a long-term care facility in Tennessee. When my friend Larry Martin and I visited her in May 2015, she eagerly told residents and care-givers in the center about the house the volunteers had built for her and Arnold.)

As I stood at Arnold's gravesite in the summer of 2014, I couldn't help but think about how far he had come since we had first met, and I couldn't help but think about how many lives he had touched. I'm certain that all those mission volunteers who cleared the lot, built the out-buildings, and built the new house will never forget the experience. I'm just as sure that those who gathered around his gravesite will never forget, either. For you see, college students from M-Fuge, the current director of M-Fuge at the University of the Cumberlands, and I dug Arnold's grave with picks and shovels. Then the M-Fuge youth carried his casket to the gravesite, and when the memorial service was over, they covered the grave with dirt.

Looking back at the entire experience, I readily admit that often I was bothered when some members of the mission groups who worked on the house were upset when things didn't go as they'd planned. On the other hand, I understood where Arnold was coming from as well. I knew it would take time for him to change.

Looking back, I know that at any point in Cedaridge's involvement we could have pulled away from Arnold and Martha. If we had, what a blessing so many people would have missed. Was the Lord's ultimate purpose for Arnold and Martha to have a safe, nice house or was it that they would get saved? Was a part of His purpose that they come to trust people again? Was a part of His purpose to show all those mission groups that in life things don't always go as planned, but in the end God will be glorified? Was the Lord's purpose all of these things and more that only He knows? And what a blessing Angie and all the M-Fuge students would have missed had Arnold and Martha's new house been completed on our timetable!

Over the years, I've learned that if we put too much emphasis on expectations in the beginning stages of helping someone or in the beginning stages of a ministry project, then we can easily get discouraged when our expectations aren't met. I've also learned there always seems to be one or two people on a mission team who don't understand that sometimes Cedaridge can't have everything in perfect order when the team arrives; often, we run out of money or we run out of volunteers to get the pre-project work done. Some volunteers and even some of the people we help don't understand that while the framing of a house is usually a quick job, the inside finish work takes much longer. Simply put, it takes time to build a house from the ground up. Sometimes people question how Cedaridge selects the people we help. For me, in order to handle such issues I must know God wants Cedaridge to build each house. (Frankly, it's much easier to remodel than to build from scratch.)

The lesson, then, is to do what the Lord puts at hand, stay focused, and wait to see what He will do in His time and in His way. The blessings will always be much greater than we could ever have expected.

I'M OFTEN ASKED if having a livable house makes any real difference in people's lives. Actually, I'm amazed at the difference in people when they move into a house we've remodeled or built from scratch. It's as though I'm watching them change before my very eyes, even as I'm watching the house go up. Hopes are rebuilt; dreams are re-dreamed; the future looks brighter.

You know, living in a house that isn't worth fixing up is very depressing – you know whatever you do will only be a temporary fix. The house will just get worse later. Plus, most of the families with whom we work aren't physically or financially able to make the needed repairs. So, they fall into a downward spiral with no hope of recovery. And then those mission groups – those missionaries – come along and tell them, "We want to give you a better place to live." What a blessing! What a privilege!

AS CEDARIDGE GREW and branched out, our board members and I often talked about our purpose. Looking back, it seems that since about 1994 the two constants have been the distribution of food and other goods and the building and repairing of houses. But most importantly, we have never lost sight of the primary purpose of the ministry, and that is to point people to Jesus.

---

LOOKING IN: *Cathy Edwards*

*On July 14, 1996, thirty-one youth filled a church bus and headed to Barbourville, Kentucky. Excitement filled the air. None of us – including the adults on the trip – had ever ventured out to tackle a project like this. Simply put: We were going to build a house for a very deserving lady. That's all we knew; details would come later. We knew she was a Christian and had lived her life serving others.*

*Upon our arrival, expectations of what we would learn and achieve as a group were high. What did God have in store for us? How would this adventure change our lives? Meeting Manda (she pronounced it "Mandy") and seeing her house was first on our to-do list. When I first saw her, she seemed rather smaller and younger than I had expected. She was charming, with a smile that went from ear to ear. Touring what she called her home was eye opening for all of us. Her home had a leaky roof, walls lined with cardboard for insulation, and an extension cord that ran from a neighboring home to provide electricity.*

*Yes, we were going to build Mandy a new home, and we did just that. Our youth completed the house in one week, but we all will carry the lessons we learned that week for the rest of our lives. We learned how to share; we learned new skills; we learned how to appreciate the things God gives us.*

*At church we hear sermons about what we as Christians should do, but putting our feet forward and actually doing what the Bible says became reality as we built Mandy a new house. She was so very proud of that house that each afternoon after our work crew had left, she would go to her soon-to-be home and sweep and clean each room.*

*"Therefore, as we have opportunity, let us do good to all people, especially to those who belong to the family of believers" (Galatians 6:10, NIV).*

*May God bless you, Mandy, for giving us the opportunity to serve and the willingness to step out of the box to do something different.*

David and Cathy Edwards
Mission Team Members
Shadowbrook Baptist Church
Suwanee, Georgia
July 1996
(Remembrances written in 2015)

LOOKING IN: *Bruce Byce*
*Kathy and I had come to Cedaridge to talk with Keith about what Mission Development Ministries planned to provide for needy families in the area for Christmas. After we had talked a long while, I (Bruce) felt the Lord leading me to ask him what he planned to provide for his own family. In true Keith fashion, he replied, "Our blessing is helping other people."*

*I then asked, "What about your girls? Have they mentioned anything they want? What can we do for them?"*

*By the time we had been together for a couple of hours, Kathy and I realized that no Christmas was coming to the Decker household that year. So we went back to South Carolina and gathered lots of things so they could have a really good Christmas. They were so grateful.*

*Keith's life philosophy is "everything is going to be all right." He had nothing for his children, but he wouldn't stop talking about how he and his family were helping others.*

*Come to think of it, he probably knew God would provide. He just didn't know when.*

*And you know what? You can't help but catch Keith's faith.*

Bruce Byce
Mission Development Ministries
Anderson, South Carolina

# Seven

In February 2012 as I was thinking about all the ways God had blessed Cedaridge Ministries, I was feeling great pride in what He had accomplished when all of a sudden the Lord spoke to my heart. *"Son,"* He said, *"what I have done in the past will not even be a shadow of what I'm doing now and what I'm getting ready to do."* It was an awesome moment.

Over the years the Lord had shown Himself strong on behalf of our ministry many, many times. What more would He do, I wondered. Only He knew.

That day as I reflected on the fifteen years Cedaridge had been located in the Bailey Building, I thanked the Lord that He had taken care of the two headaches that had caused us the most pain: The roof had needed to be replaced and the basement had desperately needed to be waterproofed. Thankfully, soon after we'd moved to the building in 1996, Christian Appalachian Project had given us a grant that was matched by the Kentucky Baptist Convention to pay for the materials to put a tin roof on the entire building. A group of eighth-grade girls, their leaders, another man, and I had put on the tin, which came in fifty-two-foot sheets. I was so grateful for the tin that I'd even prayed for rain, and when the rain came I'd stood outside and watched it pour off the roof and thanked the Lord that it didn't pour into the building anymore. Unfortunately, the tin roof had merely been a stop-gap measure since we hadn't had the money to remove the existing roof and underlying rotting joists and boards, which left the building with extreme dampness and mold and all the problems that I wrote about in previous chapters.

As for the basement waterproofing, after several years in the building Second Baptist Church in Granite, Illinois, had given us $5,500 to waterproof a portion of the basement, and then, thanks to the generosity of the local company that did the waterproofing, we had been able to waterproof the entire basement, not just a part of it. No longer had it been necessary for Joyce and me to spend two-hour stretches vacuuming water from the basement after every hard rain.

I thought about how things had been looking better for Cedaridge until a tornado hit our area in 2007 and we had lost a significant portion of our roof. We hadn't had insurance on the building and hadn't known where to turn or what to do. We had been devastated.

And just as quickly I thought about how even in the midst of the tornado, the Lord had not forgotten us: A mission group that had been in the area when the tornado struck had come to Cedaridge that very day and removed the torn tin and covered the roof with tarps. As the Lord would have it, one member of the group was a commercial roofer who'd known exactly what to do.

I reflected on how later that week when I'd gone to our banker to tell him the situation, he had said there was nothing that the bank could do. I remembered how when I'd told Joyce, despair had filled her face. As for me, I'd been very discouraged and had desperately listened for a word from the Lord. With the roof off, I'd known more water than ever before would pour into the building. I remembered how that week the only word I'd heard from the Lord had been, *"Take pictures,"* and I had obeyed.

I reflected on how that hadn't been the end of the story – the Lord had given me a word through another banker-friend. When I'd told him the situation, he'd said he would call our banker and ask him to look into the matter again. The next word I'd heard was good news: Because Cedaridge still carried a mortgage on the building, the bank carried insurance on it. As for the earlier word from the Lord to *"Take pictures,"* it was those pictures that convinced the bank to pay. The bottom line: We would have enough money from the insurance to pay off the mortgage on the building.

As I reflected, I chuckled a bit as I remembered how I'd bought $700 worth of tin of various colors to cover the damaged areas of the roof and then put it on. Again, it had been a stop-gap measure, but at least we were dry.

As I reflected, I thanked the Lord that by the end of 2007, Cedaridge was debt-free. Once again, the Lord had heard our cry from the mountains and shown Himself strong on our behalf.

More memories flooded my soul. In 2009 we'd been able to do a more permanent fix of the roof when we'd received a $54,000 grant. Volunteers had removed the entire roof down to the concrete blocks, replaced the rotten joists, and re-roofed the entire building. Dewey and Kathy Akin from the Southern Baptist Appalachian Regional Ministries had enlisted the volunteers. An added bonus had come in that the grant included money to replace our worn-out forklift, which we'd bought in 1993.

THAT FEBRUARY day in 2012 as I reflected on God's goodness to Cedaridge, I recalled how over the spring and summer of 2011 local and out-of-state volunteer groups along with students from the University of the Cumberlands and Eastern Kentucky University in Richmond had remodeled the old Bailey Building, logging more than 3,500 volunteer hours in the process. They'd reworked our kitchen, added two new showers and a toilet, added more beds to the dorms so that we could house forty-five volunteers, and added smoke alarms. One college group from Eastern had even come back three days a week for several weeks to mow grass, paint, and work in the recycling center.

I thought about how our Country Store/thrift shop was doing better than it had ever done, which meant that more people were getting much-needed supplies. Plus, the store was netting enough profit to help pay our utilities and other operating expenses. I praised the Lord that we were up-to-date on our utility bills.

I thought about how we were providing places of employment for three people through the local Experience Works federal government program and for two people through the city of Williamsburg. I thought about the six people who had worked off more than 1,600 community-service hours through Cedaridge Ministries.

I thanked the Lord for our partnership with several area churches and organizations in hosting two-day Give-A-Way events at both the Corn Creek Community Center and at the Canada Town Community Center. I thanked Him for the opportunity to share the gospel at each event.

As I reflected on the past years, I felt we were in better shape for ministry than ever before. The Lord had been good to us, seeing us through the hard times and leading us to an easier path. Now, for the first time ever, we could turn our attention to improving the grounds outside the building as well as to expanding our ministries to people in the community.

THOSE, HOWEVER, were my plans, not the Lord's plans. A few months later – in October 2012, to be exact – He began revealing His future for the ministry. That month, Lonnie Anderson, a good friend who is a retired school superintendent for Whitley County Schools and a local realtor, came to see me at Cedaridge. What he asked me that day shook me.

"Would you be interested in trading the Bailey Building for another building?" Lonnie asked.

I immediately started shaking my head, "No."

But then as I started my head in the other direction to complete the "No," the Lord swelled up in me and said, *"Don't say 'no'; don't say 'yes'; just listen."*

To the Lord I said, *"Okay, Lord, it's Your ministry."*

To Lonnie I said, "Tell me what you've got."

He told me about a 42,000-square-foot warehouse on three acres in a great location off Exit 15 on Interstate 75 on Watts Creek Road. We set a date for me to see the building, which once had housed Tri-County Assemblies and more recently had housed Ayrshire Electronics. As for our Bailey property, the University of the Cumberlands wanted to purchase it to expand their holdings near the Interstate.

In the meantime, I talked with several Cedaridge Ministries board members even though I still didn't know much about the building. I knew there was a larger issue to be settled: What would the mission groups that had worked so hard and invested so much time and financial resources in remodeling the Bailey Building think about leaving it behind? I told the board members I thought the groups would be fine with the move; after all, this was something the Lord was asking us to do and not something we'd set out to do ourselves. Board members agreed not to say an immediate "No," but to listen to the Lord for the answer.

That year, when groups began to arrive for Thanksgiving and Christmas ministries, I pulled the leaders aside and asked them if they were given the opportunity to buy a building almost three times the size of the Bailey Building, all on one level, with forklift capability and four loading docks, and structurally sound, what would they do.

I talked to leaders of at least ten returning groups. Some were hesitant to give their opinion and some felt we were making a bad move. When they saw the proposed new building, however, to a person every leader of a returning group was on board.

I especially remember the response of an eighty-plus-year-old woman from Tennessee, "I would jump at it in a second – you are maxed out here," Jeanette Thomas said.

For at least five years, Mrs. Thomas had led teams with as many as seventy-two volunteers from Wallace Memorial Baptist Church in Knoxville to come to minister through Cedaridge. The groups had brought food to distribute and had worked in our clothes closet and food pantry; they had run a temporary nurse's station and temporary beauty shop for area women; they had worked on constructing homes for needy people in the community. Often, on a two-day trip, they had served as many as 600 people. Mrs. Thomas was very familiar with the limitations of the Bailey Building, even after it had been remodeled. I trusted her judgment, too, because all you have to do is be around her for a short time and you know she is close to the Lord.

When Mrs. Thomas left my office, in my mind I began to walk through the ministry and our space. For the first time, I realized we were maxed out, as she had said. If we were ever to expand, we would need more space.

The deal was sealed for me when I asked the leader of another group who had worked on the remodeling about moving. He said, "We weren't working on a building; we were working for the Lord."

Cedaridge board members worked through their misgivings, too. When I first had asked the board's secretary, Brenda Mack, what she thought about the move, she had responded, "Keith, what are you thinking about? Volunteers have just remodeled the building; they've put in new showers; they've put in new dorms." Those were legitimate concerns, of course. I then had asked her, "Sister Brenda, is this God's building or our building?" That's all it took for her to get on board. Soon all the board members were on board, too.

WITHIN A FEW months of Mr. Anderson's initial conversation with me, Cedaridge had moved into the building. After almost seventeen years at the Bailey Building, we had a new home in which all our ministries could be under one roof and in a structurally sound building that would accommodate expanding ministries. Plus, there were no water or mold problems.

It was amazing how quickly the Lord had worked everything out. It was even more amazing how He did it. The Cedaridge board signed the papers to buy the building on Nov. 05, 2012. With the help of five out-of-state volunteer groups, we moved in March 2013. It was the fifth move for Cedaridge Ministries since our beginning twenty-one years before. As with each previous move, the Lord had required a step of faith: Either the ministry would fold or move forward with Him.

We moved in debt-free. With the money from the sale of the Bailey Building, we were able to pay off the indebtedness on the new building, put money aside for future needs, and put some into Cedaridge's general operating fund. God was good. Thanks to additional funds provided by mission groups, we also were able to take care of repair issues at our new property, such as repairing a leak in the building's roof, redoing the gutters, and building a covered porch the length of the entire backside of the building.

On May 03 and 04, we held our ribbon cutting and grand opening and invited people whom we serve to attend. Thanks to volunteers from Victory Baptist Church in Corbin, Kentucky, and Concord First Baptist Church in Knoxville, Tennessee, we had a glorious time. The Concord group provided a family fun festival party complete with food, face painting, and inflatables, and their seventy-member youth group gave a gospel concert and led worship services.

LOOKING BACK at the two years we've been at the Watts Creek Road site, I can already see how the Lord is working to move Cedaridge forward. Now in early 2015, we have the following ministries:

*Food Distribution.* We've begun to get back on track with receiving and distributing semi-loads of food and materials. By the time we moved from the Bailey Building, we were receiving only fifteen loads per year. In 2013, with four loading docks we were able to receive twenty-five loads. In 2014, we received thirty loads. We aren't yet back to pre-recession levels, but we're working hard to renew our relationships and build new relationships with suppliers. Over the years, I've learned it takes about three years to build trust with companies and organizations that want to make donations. Getting back to our past levels will take time. Because the Watts Creek Road building is easily accessible for semis and the interior space is large, we also can hold on-site Give-A-Way events when truckloads of goods arrive.

I'm often asked how we learn about the availability of large shipments of food and other items. Sometimes another helping agency will contact us when they have things available. Sometimes a member of a church mission group works for a company that gives items to charities. Sometimes a truck driver is a member of a mission group and wants to be available to pick up loads for us. Sometimes it is simply word-of-mouth.

Also, for many years Mission of Hope, an Appalachian relief ministry that serves depressed communities in Northeast Tennessee, Southeast Kentucky, and Southwest Virginia, has funneled thousands of pounds of goods through Cedaridge. Mission of Hope and its executive director, Emmette Thompson, have been steady partners through all these years.

We continue to rely on the churches and ministries to whom we give the goods to vet the recipients. In order to be fair to all the churches and ministries with which we work, we rotate the distributions, making sure that organizations large and small get a piece of the pie. Some of those groups may serve 500 people; some twenty. For example, many of the smaller churches in the area don't have the resources or space to house a food pantry, so they use Cedaridge's pantry. In 2014, in conjunction with our ministry partners, Cedaridge helped feed more than 5,000 families each month.

*Projects for Mission Groups.* In the summer of 2013, we hosted and worked with seventy-two out-of-area mission groups, some of whom stayed in our newly built on-site dorms and prepared their meals in our new kitchen. The groups did everything from building projects to hosting block parties at our property to clean-up to conducting Vacation Bible School and leading worship services. In 2014, we hosted and worked with seventy-eight out-of-area mission groups. Groups ranged in size from twenty to seventy people.

*In-House Ministries.* Because of the additional space in the Watts Creek Road building, we've been able to expand our in-house ministries. Those ministries now include the following:

*Preacher's Closet,* filled with suits for ministers who come to the building to shop. We also pass the suits along to other ministries such as Oneida Baptist Institute, the Kentucky Baptist Convention's boarding high school in Oneida, Kentucky, and Clear Creek Baptist Bible College, a preacher's college in Pineville, Kentucky. We've sent Clear Creek as many as seventy suits at a time.

*Food Pantry,* stocked with staples that needy people can receive any day Cedaridge is open. Area churches use the pantry, too. We use money that we receive from Southern Baptist Convention hunger funds to buy food to augment what we receive from other sources.

*Country Store/thrift shop,* which serves about 150 individuals each week. Mission of Hope in Knoxville, Tenn., regularly brings truckloads of clothing to be distributed through the Country Store.

*Sister's Keeper Shop* provides maternity clothes and baby items to needy mothers and mothers-to-be. We also pass on items from the shop to area pregnancy centers, family resource centers, and health service centers. In 2014, when we received a semi-load of items from Dignity Wear, a manufacturer of maternity and baby clothes, we were able to store the items in our new building. We couldn't have done that at the Bailey Building. Out-of-area women also crochet and knit baby clothes to be given away in the shop. A woman in Georgia oversees this ministry. We always give each person who uses the shop a Bible, and we talk with each one of them about the Lord.

*Christian Literature Distribution,* begun by the Southern Baptist Appalachian Regional Ministries (ARM). ARM and Cross Ministries in Knoxville, Tennessee, give us Bibles and Christian literature to distribute on-site or to pass on to area churches.

*Backpack Distribution,* in conjunction with Appalachian Regional Ministries. In December 2013, Cedaridge hosted a party at which 1,700 backpacks filled with clothing, school supplies, and toys were distributed. The backpacks and their contents were valued at about $75 each.

One young single mom said she came because with Christmas coming she knew she needed help. She added that what she especially appreciated was the dignity with which she and her children were treated. She said that allowed her not to feel ashamed to ask for help.

That day, sixty people came to faith in Christ as the Gospel was shared.

In December 2014, about 2,000 people representing 484 families attended the backpack distribution event. More than 200 volunteers served the people. About 1,200 backpacks were distributed, and twenty people became Christians.

*Furniture and Household Items,* which we provide for victims of major catastrophes, such as loss of homes through fire. With the expanded space,

Cedaridge now can store such items under dry, safe conditions. Mission of Hope regularly brings truckloads of furniture and household items for us to pass on to needy people.

*Church Furniture,* which we give to churches to use to furnish pastors' studies and church offices. We also provide chairs for Sunday School rooms.

*Church Supplies* such as Vacation Bible School materials for churches that can't afford to purchase them.

*Weekday Noon Meals,* which Joyce cooks for our local volunteers. Money is provided through Southern Baptist hunger funds.

*Meals for Mission Teams,* prepared by Joyce.

*Block Parties,* such as Vacation Bible School block parties and Christmas Give-A-Way block parties. A local company provides inflatables and food for many of these events. We now can safely hold these parties on the grounds of our new facility.

*Annual Autumn Events,* which provide needed supplies for area families. For the last four years, Mission of Hope has come to Cedaridge for an October event at which they distribute food, clothing, hygiene items, household items, toys, school supplies, and Bible tracts to as many as 500 families. Group members always share Christ one-on-one; each year people get saved or rededicate themselves to the Lord.

Before the move to the Watts Creek Road building, the event was held at the Williamsburg Tourism and Convention Center. Now, we use a third building that Cedaridge leased in 2014 on our Watts Creek Road site. We give left-over items from these autumn events to local school family resource centers for distribution or store them until we can deliver them to families who can't get to the event.

*Thanksgiving Events.* In 2014, Bismarck Baptist Church in Bismarck, Mo., along with Southpark Baptist Church in Corbin, Corn Creek Baptist Church in Woodbine, and Watts Chapel in Williamsburg, held two Thanksgiving Give-A-Way events. One was held at the Cedaridge building and served 320 families. The other was held in Jackson County and served 125 families. The Missouri church provided half of the financing for the events as well. (Other church mission groups also host similar events.)

*Christmas Events.* In December 2013, at the ARM Christmas backpack distribution event mentioned above, 560 food boxes were distributed. Everyone who came was also treated to lunch.

For the last five years, Whitesburg Baptist Church in Huntsville, Ala., has sponsored a Christmas Give-A-Way event. A pig roast, inflatables, and games add to the festive atmosphere. At the December 2014 event, 1,200 people came and were served by sixty volunteers. Most importantly, seventeen people got saved. (Other church mission groups host similar events.) Whitesburg Church also brings a volunteer group to Cedaridge each summer.

*Recycling.* Cedaridge's re-cycling program, which serves the community, was located in the new Watts Creek Road building for about a year until the Lord opened the opportunity for a lease-purchase of the 70,000-square-feet Tri-County Assembly Building and ten-plus acres at the back of our building. This was a God-send because the recycling operation had grown three times larger than it had been at the Bailey Building. We moved the entire recycling operation there in March 2014. Volunteer Robert "Bob" Frost headed up the operation for about a year until illness forced him to resign. Now, Holly Decker, our daughter, directs this ministry.

*Bunks and Showers for Volunteer Mission Groups.* We can accommodate 250 people in our bunks. We charge a nominal fee per night, which goes into Cedaridge's operating budget. Of the seventy-eight mission groups that Cedaridge hosted in 2014, sixty-five were housed in our new facility.

*Sharing the Gospel.* We share Jesus every time we have an opportunity and regularly see people accept Jesus as Savior. For example, at the December 2013 backpack distribution event mentioned above, sixty people made professions of faith in Jesus as Lord.

WHEN WE WERE preparing to move into the Watts Creek Road facility, several people asked me where I planned to put my office. To tell the truth, I hadn't even thought about that. As I began to think about it, I realized there was one thing I really wanted: I wanted Joyce to have an office next door to mine. When I toured the building with that in mind, I was amazed at what I found: The most suitable spot for my office had a room off it that would be perfect for Joyce. Plus, there was no door – just an opening – between the two rooms, which meant we could enjoy watching each other work.

The Lord had provided just what we need because He knows that Joyce is such a vital partner in the ministry. Even after thirty-eight years of being together, we want to be with each other more than ever. We need each other, and our best ideas come when we share with each other. Joyce is at Cedaridge almost every day we are open, doing any and everything that needs to be done. Most any day you will find her cooking, cleaning, managing and working in the Country Store, or talking with people – or in her office next to mine, tending to the details of the ministry.

After our children were older, Joyce had become treasurer of the ministry. She followed Fanny Taylor, who was Dad Teague's niece, and who had overseen the purchase of the Bailey Building and was gifted in business matters. While Fanny was treasurer, Joyce worked with her and did the day-to-day bill paying. Then, the board elected Joyce as treasurer and she has continued in that role to this day.

Looking back over the years, I know Joyce has an anointing to be the treasurer of the ministry, even as I have the anointing to be the overseer and to see the vision of what God wants Cedaridge to be and do. Due to her nature, Joyce does get discouraged from time to time with the precariousness of Cedaridge's financial situation. Yet, anytime I've tried to take some of the pressure off her by getting someone to help her, it hasn't worked out. The Lord has told me He isn't going to bless my efforts no matter how much I want to help her. He has told me Joyce has to deal with it herself and in her way. The Lord has told me it's hers.

Looking back from my vantage point in 2015, I'm beginning to see the fruits of Joyce's anointing as treasurer. Through the years, she has gained confidence. Now, she gets her own word from the Lord, including the word that the Lord will take care of everything.

I also must write a word about Joyce and her ministry in the Country Store/thrift shop. She has always loved to talk about the Lord with the people who use the store. One day one of the regulars told Joyce that a doctor had just told her sick husband that nothing more could be done for him. The woman also told Joyce her husband was lost and asked Joyce if I would talk with him.

Later that day, as I was pulling into our parking lot Joyce came out to tell me the story – just as the couple pulled up. I immediately went over and asked the man if I could talk with him. He said I could. I told him I'd heard he wasn't saved and I asked him if he died right then, would he go to heaven. He said, "No." When I asked if he would like to go to heaven, he said, "Yes." He got saved right there.

Then there's the rest of the story. The man got saved on Friday. He went back to see his doctor the following Tuesday. After examining him, the doctor said, "Something's happened to you." The man replied, "Yes, I know. I got saved and I'm on my way to heaven." The doctor then told him he was talking about his heart – something had happened to it since the previous

Friday's appointment. The doctor told the man when he'd examined him that day, he'd felt the man's heart couldn't be fixed – that's why he had told the man and his wife there was nothing more that could be done. But now, at this second appointment, the doctor told the man he had a heart that didn't need fixing – he couldn't find anything wrong with the man's heart!

After that second appointment, the couple came back to Cedaridge just as I had walked outside. The wife was glowing as she hurried over to me. I'll never forget her words: "Keith, Keith, I've got something to tell you. Wait, no, I want my husband to tell you." And then he told me all the whole story. What a day of praising the Lord!

CEDARIDGE MINISTRIES has always been driven by the desire to meet the physical and spiritual needs of people in our communities. Often, as has been shown throughout this book, that has led to the Lord directing us to forms of ministry that we could never have planned or envisioned ourselves. Never has that been truer than with the opening of satellite operations in several neighboring communities in recent years. Because of the downturn in the economy, many people didn't have money to buy gasoline to drive to Williamsburg to the Cedaridge facility, and so we began satellite ministries in Barbourville, Canada Town, and Woodbine and are working toward a fourth in Jackson County. Each is a mini-Cedaridge operated by people from the local community. Cedaridge, along with other helping entities and interested people, provides the goods that the centers distribute.

The story of how the first satellite center began is yet another illustration of how the Lord has worked. Betty Swafford gave her permission for the story to be included in this book.

### Boyd Swafford

ONE DAY a preacher-friend asked me to go with him to visit a man named Noah who was very sick. We went, prayed with Noah, and rejoiced to see Noah get saved that day. After we left Noah's home, as we were passing the home of Boyd and Betty Swafford my friend said, "There's somebody we need to pray for." He was referring to Boyd, who was his brother-in-law.

I said, "Let's put Boyd in Noah's place on our prayer list, since Noah just got saved," and he agreed.

We had barely made it to the bottom of the hill below the Swaffords' house when my preacher-friend received a call from Betty. "Boyd's in the bedroom, praying," she said. We looked at each other and realized that God was at work. Not long after, Boyd got saved.

Looking back in 2015, "Getting saved changed my husband's life," Betty says. His salvation was a strong witness to many people in the community. In fact, Betty says his baptism at Corn Creek Baptist Church was scheduled on a night the local football team was playing, but when the church youth insisted that they wanted to attend the baptism, the church changed the date.

Later when I went back to visit Boyd, he said that because he was now saved he needed to take care of a couple of things. First, he was known as the biggest bootlegger in the community and he knew he had to do something about that. And he did. Second, he also was known for his foul language. That, too, changed. "If God was big enough to save me, He's also big enough to take that filthy mouth from me, too," he said.

Still later Boyd asked me what he could do for Cedaridge. When I told him I'd like to have a building he owned in Woodbine to start a satellite mini-Cedaridge ministry, his first question was, "When do you want it?"

In 2007, Betty became the ministry director of the Woodbine Corn Creek Center with Boyd helping out. "He didn't know he could have a life so good," Betty says. "He came down to the center even in the dead of winter." Boyd was a great supporter of the ministry until his death about three years later.

Today, Betty continues to direct the center. You will find her there five days a week, giving out food, clothing, and lots of love. "There are so many stories and all of them touch my heart," she says. "The needs are great; the situations are bad." And she always tells the people that first and foremost they need God; she tells them to go to church. After all, she knows first-hand how that can change a life.

OVER THE YEARS the number of churches and organizations with which Cedaridge works has settled in to about 400. In 2015, the area we serve includes nine counties: Bell, Clay, Jackson, Knox, Laurel, McCreary, and Whitley in Kentucky; and Campbell and Knox in Tennessee. According to the U.S. Census, in 2012 the total population of those nine counties was 270,435.[1]

True to our original purpose, Cedaridge continues to serve as a distribution point for many large shipments of food and supplies. We estimate that we have distributed between 17 and 18 million pounds of food over the years.

Over the years, we've hosted and worked with volunteer groups that have built more than 100 homes. Each year since we began working in housing those volunteers have remodeled an average of five to six homes and made minor repairs to about 300 other homes. My heart fills with joy each time I participate in the dedication of a home. One in particular stands out in my memory. One of the volunteers who had worked on the house led a brief service in which he read Scripture and dedicated the house to the Lord. He told the owners that all he and the other volunteers had done was to physically build a house, but now they were praying that the owners would accept God's gift of eternal life and live for Him. He then presented the owners a Bible. The dedication concluded with the home owners pickin' and singin' the song "I Saw the Light."

Sadly, the needs in Eastern Kentucky are as great as they were when Cedaridge Ministries began more than twenty years ago. Of the nine counties we serve, six are among the 100 poorest in the United States. By some estimates, 46 percent of the housing in the region is substandard.[2]

In parts of the region, 20 percent of the residents don't know where their next meal is coming from. The government labels them as "food insecure," meaning they are often unable to afford the food they need.[3]

I'm often asked why I continue with the ministry when the needs seem as great as they were when Cedaridge began more than two decades ago. My answer is that this is what God has called me to do and until He tells me to quit, I'll continue on. I've learned I don't serve because of what I see with my own eyes or even how I feel, but I serve wholly based on what the Lord desires. I know He has a plan and He knows what He is doing, and as long as I do what He wants, I get to be a part of that plan. In the end, it will be well worth it all. Jesus said, "Inasmuch as ye have done it unto one of the least of these my brethren, ye have done it unto me" (Matthew 25:40, KJV). I love doing things for Jesus, and according to this Scripture, I know I can do things that make Him happy. I also shudder to think what would have happened to many of the people we've helped had Cedaridge not existed.

I'M ALSO OFTEN asked what Cedaridge needs. We always need money for our operating budget. Utilities, maintenance, and insurance are major expenses.

We always need volunteers for the day-to-day, week-in-and-week-out work in the Country Store/thrift shop. We need volunteers who can load and unload materials and clean the inside and outside of the Cedaridge facilities. Mowing, edging, and sprucing up the grounds as well as maintaining our vehicles are constant needs. A few volunteer hours make a big difference.

We need mission groups who can go into the community to do minor and major home repairs, build new structures to replace substandard houses, and conduct Bible schools and block parties. We always count on mission groups to help us with our Thanksgiving and Christmas Give-A-Way events each year.

And most importantly, we need Christians who can tell people the good news about Jesus and His love. We need Christians who will pray that the Lord will continue to hear our cry from the mountains.

---

LOOKING IN: *Bruce Byce*

*We had just completed a week-long mission project with a team we had brought from South Carolina to work at Cedaridge. After the team left, Kathy and I stayed behind to meet another team from the coastal area of South Carolina that hadn't been to Cedaridge before. While we were waiting, Keith asked if we could follow him to a nearby town to return a rental truck he had been using.*

*It was a sunny afternoon when we left and headed north on I-75. About twenty minutes into our drive, dark clouds rolled in over the mountains and the rain and wind started. It was almost impossible to see, but we were afraid to pull over, fearing that other drivers would not be able to see our vehicle.*

*After Keith dropped off the rental truck, he got in our car and said that his wife, Joyce, had just called to tell him that the storm had hit the Cedaridge building in Williamsburg and had torn off part of the roof.*

*We headed back south on I-75 as fast as we could, only to find traffic blocked because of overturned vehicles. As we sat in the car and prayed, we repeatedly asked Keith what he thought he should do. Each time we asked, his reply was the same, "God is telling me to take pictures."*

*We finally made our way back to Cedaridge, and what we saw was bad. Keith just kept saying that God was telling him to take pictures, so Kathy handed him her camera and he got on his cherry picker and as he went up to the roof, he took lots of pictures. We had the film developed and gave the pictures to Keith.*

*As the Lord would have it, another volunteer group was in the area that day and had a commercial roofer on their team. They came over and knew just what to do. They removed the torn tin and secured the roof with tarps.*

*As we all stood in front of the Cedaridge building and we held hands and prayed with those volunteers whom we had not met before, there was a sweet presence of the Lord in our midst that was bringing peace in a time of disaster. You don't forget moments like that.*

Bruce Byce
President
Mission Development Ministries
Anderson, South Carolina

LOOKING IN: *Emmette Thompson*

*At Mission of Hope, we look for mountain ministry centers like Cedaridge Ministries to help them serve people in their community who are in dire need. When we first met Brother Keith Decker and his wife, Joyce, a few years ago, we realized immediately that they were extremely humble servant-driven folk. Over the years since then, we have watched them as they have lived out their faith and have been vessels of Hope for many people in their community and beyond who have lost all Hope. We have watched how God has blessed their ministry and their efforts with His hand of provision. And they, in turn, have given Him all the praise.*

*At Mission of Hope, we feel that God's true front line in the trenches, the foot soldiers in rural Appalachia, are sweet-spirited Christians like Keith and Joyce Decker. It is an honor and a privilege to work alongside them. And we pray that God will watch over them and bless them each and every day.*

Emmette Thompson
Executive Director
Mission of Hope
Knoxville, Tennessee

LOOKING IN: *Teresa Parrett*

*Keith has a heart for serving the less fortunate and is one of the most humble persons I have ever met. Literally thousands of impoverished children and families have been touched through his ministry. And with every food box or toy that is given out, every home repair that is done, every contact that is made, Keith is quick to remind those he serves that it is all about Jesus. He takes no credit for anything that has been accomplished. All praise and glory go to God.*

*Many times Keith and Joyce have sacrificed their own comfort to provide for the physical and spiritual needs of others. It is impossible to calculate this side of eternity the number of persons who have come to know the Lord through the outreach of Keith and Joyce and Cedaridge.*

*In 2014, the Kentucky Baptist Convention recognized Keith's commitment and effectiveness in evangelism and ministry and his demonstration of going the second mile by naming him the Kentucky Baptist Missionary of the Year. He is most deserving.*

Teresa Parrett
Missions Mobilization Coordinator
Kentucky Baptist Convention
Louisville, Kentucky

LOOKING IN: *Brenda Mack*

*I have known Joyce Decker since high school. Keith and Joyce also attended my family's church on occasion as I was growing up. I remember them visiting our church during revivals and other occasions.*

*Joyce is, and always has been, Keith's biggest supporter and right arm. She is his quiet strength. Joyce has been a faithful worker, wife, and mother. She has been a friend to a lot of people. She always has a smile and is always willing to help out with anything that needs to be done at Cedaridge. She often goes the extra mile. In fact, for weeks at a time during the busy summer months, she regularly gets up at 3:30 in the morning to go to the ministry building to cook for mission groups that have come to work with Cedaridge.*

*I appreciate her friendship.*

Brenda Mack
Secretary
Cedaridge Board of Directors
Williamsburg, Kentucky

# Eight

O ver the years some people have questioned why I don't make decisions about the ministry and about my life until I hear a clear word from the Lord. Often, they expect me to respond on the spur of the moment to something they think I should be doing or to do long-range planning for the ministry. That's just not what I believe the Lord has ever wanted for Cedaridge as a faith-driven ministry.

The way I see it, if you trust that the Lord knows what He wants to do, then He's going to tell you. It's that simple. Then you have the joy of watching the Lord work because you have given Him the reins to set the boundaries instead of beginning with boundaries you've set yourself. The joy comes when you keep yourself in check and just watch for what God is doing and listen for His word of direction to you. Proverbs 3:5-6 says, "Trust in the LORD with all thine heart and lean not on thine own understanding. In all thy ways acknowledge him, and he shall direct thy paths" (KJV). And Jeremiah 29:11 says that the Lord knows the plans He has for us – and that is for us to prosper and to hope.

Long ago I learned I must wait for a direct word from God or I will make a mess of things. I know Cedaridge has lost some supporters because of this, but I can't worry about that. I must follow the Lord.

From the day of my baptism, I've felt the Lord continuing to tell me that I must "walk that lonesome valley" by myself. That day, I'd learned a principle that would guide me throughout my life: You don't need to check with others about what you need to do when the Lord has already made it clear what you are to do. Through the years, I've always tried to be understanding and listen to advice; I've always sought out people who have proven they let the Lord lead them and I've been encouraged by their advice. But I've always believed the Lord doesn't want me to share everything about the ministry with everyone. There are some burdens that do not need to be placed on the shoulders of others and there are some burdens that other people simply will not understand; therefore, their advice would only make things more difficult. Through the years, I've always believed the final decision must come from the person or persons who will be held accountable for the decision. And, most importantly, I've always believed it is very important to make sure it is the Lord who is telling you what to do. Once you know that, you do only what He has asked.

I know, too, that at first glance some people are mystified at my leadership style and at the seemingly disorganized way in which Cedaridge functions, but I've heard enough positive stories to know that many of those same people come around to praising the Lord for what He accomplishes by the time they complete a mission project with us. (I also know some people have never come around.)

Long-time supporters Bruce and Kathy Byce of Anderson, South Carolina, have seen this occur many times over the thirteen years they've been involved with Cedaridge, even as they have experienced the frustration that comes from my leadership style. Kathy recounts this story:

> *One Easter week, we brought a group from South Carolina for their first mission trip to Cedaridge. They were scheduled to distribute food boxes to needy people in the community. We had asked Keith to have everything organized before we arrived. When we got to Cedaridge, it was seed potato day and dozens of people were lined up at the Bailey Building to receive free seed potatoes for their spring plantings.*
>
> *Keith took us over to meet a man who was sitting on a wall by himself. Turns out, it was Wilbur, a local pastor whom Keith said we should visit on our way to distribute the food boxes.*
>
> *We gathered our group, got in our vehicle, and started driving to what we thought would be the first stop for our food distribution. Then Keith startled us. "Bruce," he said, "Slow down. Don't drive so fast." Well, Bruce was driving at about thirty miles per hour, so he asked, "Slow down? Why?"*
>
> *Imagine our surprise and the surprise of all those first-timers in the van when Keith answered, "Because the Lord hasn't told me where our first stop is."*

*Fast-forward to the end of that day: Every stop was exactly what it was supposed to be – including when we stopped to visit Wilbur at his church.*

*It seems that sometime before that day, Wilbur had asked Keith if he could find a volunteer group that could put a restroom in his church. To that point, the church had only had an outhouse.*

*When we stopped to visit Wilbur, our team piled out of the van and looked at a closet in the church that Wilbur thought might be a good spot for the restroom. Then Keith – as only he can do – announced, "Let's build an addition to the church for the restroom."*

*The team accepted the challenge and went back to South Carolina and raised the money for the project. Later that summer, we returned and built that addition on the front of the church in four days. We didn't just add one restroom, but we added two, plus a foyer. We also added a water line and a septic tank and did an electrical power upgrade. It turned into a gigantic project, but as God so often does, He had put together just the right team with the necessary skills. In fact, one man on the team worked for the largest power company in South Carolina and had the technical skills needed for the power upgrade.*

*Each evening we held Bible school, and then on Friday night we had a cookout for the team and the church members. That night, Bruce sat beside a lady in her 30s and her four-year-old daughter. "I'm so grateful that we now have a restroom in the church," she said, "because when I attended here as a child, my mother would always tell me to be sure to go the bathroom before I left home because 'you won't like going to the outhouse.'" The young woman went on to say, "I tell my daughter the same thing. Come this winter, my girl can go to inside plumbing."*

*That Friday night at 12:05 a.m., we had our first flush.*

*An added bonus was that the people said they could use the foyer for covered-dish dinners.*

*You see, on that first trip, every stop – including Wilbur's church – was anointed. Every stop was what it was supposed to be.*

BRENDA MACK, the long-time secretary of the Cedaridge Ministries board of directors, has her own stories to tell. While she says she often is "the devil's advocate" and "shoots straight" with me, she also quickly admits that she has "eaten dirt a lot and I've admitted it."

Brenda says my operational method is "the Lord said" and "the Lord told me." She says that I "wait for clarification from the Lord, and if there is no clarification, then it wasn't meant to be." While Brenda readily admits that isn't her method of discerning God's will, she says she has learned that "when it's Keith, it's okay. I just ask him, 'What did the Lord tell you this time?' He truly lives by faith and his motto is 'God has always provided.'"

One of Brenda's favorite stories comes from the days when the ministry was located in the RC Bottling Plant:

> *I came in one day and as always, things were junky – we've always been junky. Everything was a mess. There was a hospital bed, an old EKG machine, and some other medical equipment scattered everywhere. When I asked Keith what he planned to do with the stuff, in typical Keith fashion, he replied, "I don't know, Sister Brenda."*
>
> *So I told Keith, "Okay. I'll shut up." I've had to say that to him so many times. I've learned not to argue with him, because he's usually right. (Later, I learned that he sent the things to the Society of St. Andrews, who sent them to a children's hospital overseas.)*
>
> *While Keith definitely spreads himself too thin and is scattered much of the time, I see the Lord working through him. Lots of people have been blessed by him. Etched in my mind are two people Keith helped. One day when I was visiting Keith in his office, he pulled out some pictures of the two. "Sister Brenda," he said, "These two were living in a shed. She slept on a pile of garbage. Their heat was a fire pit in the middle of the room. We built a house for them." That can't be topped.*
>
> *As for Keith's motivation, I think it is to see more souls added to the kingdom. "Do you know Jesus?" is his favorite question.*

I READILY ADMIT that the hardest part of my job is turning loose of things. I find it hard to delegate. I find it hard not to get over-involved in little details – just ask my volunteer administrative assistant, Martha Logan. I always feel if something doesn't get done then I've let the Lord down.

Because I'm not getting any younger, many people have told me I need to prepare for the future by at least making plans to turn some aspects of the ministry over to other people. The Lord hasn't told me that yet, so until He does, I won't. And in recent years, instead of the Lord showing me what He wants done two or three steps at a time, He just shows me one step at a time. He tells me, *"Keith, now I only have to tell you the next step and I will get us there."*

Little did I know that when Joyce Sweeney Martin and I began working on this book in March 2014 just four months later the Lord would ask me to "graduate" from being pastor of Corn Creek Baptist Church. (Instead of the word "resign" I use the word "graduate" because I feel there is much more the Lord will have me do with the good people at Corn Creek.) When I left Corn Creek, I learned that turning loose is easy when you hear a word from the Lord telling you what to do. Waiting to hear a direct word from the Lord has served me well all my life, and I'm not going to change now. (In April 2105, I became pastor of Black Oak Baptist Church near Williamsburg.)

The purpose statement of Cedaridge Ministries is still "to bring people to faith in Jesus Christ as Savior and Lord, and to honor the Lord through all that is accomplished at Cedaridge." Our mission comes from 1 John 3:16-18. It is the mandate that drives the ministry:

> *Hereby perceive we the love of God,*
> *because he laid down his life for us:*
> *and we ought to lay down our lives for the brethren.*
> *but whoso hath this world's good,*
> *and seeth his brother have need,*
> *and shutteth up his bowels of compassion from him,*
> *how dwelleth the love of God in him?*
> *My little children,*
> *let us not love in word, neither in tongue,*
> *but in deed and in truth. (KJV)*

When we moved to the Watts Creek Road facility, many people told me they knew I had to be excited about the move, but I wasn't. The Lord had told me, *"You can be happy, but you can't be excited, because this is not even the beginning of the beginning of what I have promised to do through Cedaridge Ministries."* I believe Him and I can't wait to see what He is going to do. God still hears my cry from the mountains. I want to lift Him up.

# Epilogue

When I was in elementary school – around the fifth or sixth grade I think – I began to hear the story of how I'd been given away by my father when I was six months old because of the number of children and the lack of food in our home. And then I heard about how the Lord had blessed my dad when he'd found a nurse who'd agreed to take me in. As the years passed when my teachers assigned papers to write, I often wanted to write about what I'd learned about my early years as well as what I'd experienced since that time.

That desire never left me, so much so that in my senior year in high school I felt the Lord wanted me to write my story as a way to thank all those who had invested so much in me over the years. As I thought about what to title my paper, I kept thinking about the beautiful countryside that surrounded me. I thought about how homey and simple the mountains are and about how I'd come to love and appreciate them. I thought about how the mountains had helped define me. I felt as if the Lord was showing me myself as a fragile, very sick, hungry baby. I thought about how all through the years, it was as if a cry was coming out of me and how so many people had heard my cry and had helped me. I thought about how God had heard my cry.

Down through the years since then I've learned that I was only one of a great host of children and adults who were crying in the mountains. I've seen how God has used their cries to call out caring people to help them and change their lives, too. And I've been privileged to help connect those caring people with those crying people.

Since the time of those first efforts at writing my story when I was in high school, I've felt the Lord would make a way for me to tell the story of my personal cry from the mountains and how He has answered. Now, that has happened. It is my deepest desire for this book to lift up the most important person in my life – my Lord. I want Jesus to be lifted up so that all people will be drawn to Him (John 12:32) and know hope and fulfillment. Then for each of them, his or her cry from the mountains will be the beginning and not the end.

## Endnotes: Chapter Eight

[1]  "Kentucky Population by County," "Tennessee Population by County," http.//us-places.com/ Kentucky/population by-County, htm://us-places.com/Tennessee/population-by-County, htm; accessed Nov. 08, 2014.

[2]  http://americanmoocher.com/2011/05/100 U.S. Counties with lowest per capita-income/; accessed Nov. 08, 2014.

[3]  Chris Kenning, "Appalachian Food Pantry Highlights Hunger in Kentucky," Louisville: *The Courier-Journal*, April 20, 2014, 1, 14.

For more information or to get involved in Cedaridge Ministries, contact

**Cedaridge Ministries**
300 Watts Creek Road
Williamsburg, KY 40769-0818.
www.Cedaridgeministries.org.
Phone: 606.549.1372
606.344.5533 (cell)
E-mail: KeithDecker31@gmail.com
or
visit us on Facebook.

# About the Authors

**K**eith Decker is founder and president of Cedaridge Ministries in Williamsburg, Kentucky, in the heart of Appalachia. The ministry, which he has led since 1992, is dedicated to helping meet the needs of the poor in a nine-county region of Eastern Kentucky and Eastern Tennessee. Keith's wife, **Joyce,** is an active hands-on partner in the ministry. They are the parents of two adult daughters and one adult son. Their younger daughter, Holly, works with her parents in the Cedaridge ministry.

Both Keith and Joyce attended Cumberland College (now the University of the Cumberlands) in Williamsburg, Kentucky. Keith also served as pastor of Corn Creek Baptist Church near Woodbine, Kentucky, for twenty-six years.

**Joyce Sweeney Martin** is an author, editor, and writing coach in Louisville, Kentucky, where she and her husband, Larry, live. *Cry from the Mountains* is the ninth book of which she is the author or co-author, including *Miracle in the Mountains: Experiencing the Transforming Power of Faith in the Heart of Appalachia* with Lonnie and Belinda Riley; *Called! Step by* Step with June Hall McNeely; and *Faith Works: Ministry Models for a Hurting World.*

CPSIA information can be obtained at www.ICGtesting.com
Printed in the USA
LVOW11s0058100615

441793LV00002B/3/P